*H*eart *S*ongs
^{for}*A*nimal
*L*overs

**True Stories of Devotion,
Courage, and Love**

Collected by Hester Mundis
Foreword by Jack Hanna

Daybreak Books
An Imprint of Rodale Books
Emmaus, Pennsylvania

To the Chester Zoo,
for all you did, for all you've done, for all you do for Boris.

And in memory of Chris Lawson, D.V.M.,
who crossed the Rainbow Bridge too soon.

Copyright © 1999 Hester Mundis
Illustrations copyright © 1999 by Kathy Rusynyk

Daybreak is a registered trademark of Rodale Press, Inc.
Printed in the United States of America on acid-free ∞ , recycled paper ♻

Book Designer: Kristen Morgan Downey
Illustrator: Kathy Rusynyk

Library of Congress Cataloging-in-Publication Data

Mundis, Hester.
    Heart songs for animal lovers : true stories of devotion, courage,
and love / collected by Hester Mundis ; foreword by Jack Hanna.
        p.   cm.
    ISBN 1–57954–043–0   hardcover
    1. Pets—Anecdotes.   2. Domestic animals—Anecdotes.   3. Pet owners—
Anecdotes.   4. Human-animal relationships—Anecdotes.   I. Title.
SF416.M86   1999
636.088'7—dc21   99–16372

Distributed to the book trade by St. Martin's Press

2   4   6   8   10   9   7   5   3   1   hardcover

Visit us on the Web at www.rodalebooks.com, or call us toll-free at (800) 848-4735.

--- OUR PURPOSE ---

We publish books that empower
people's minds and spirits.

Acknowledgments

All the people and animals I encountered in the course of writing this book expanded my world in wise and lasting ways, for which I am enormously grateful. But there are some individuals, organizations, publications, and institutions that were invaluable in enabling me to locate sources and obtain stories, and, therefore, deserve special mention, gratitude, and recognition for their help in the completion of this project.

My sincere thanks to the Delta Society for hooking me up to their extraordinary network of storytellers; Dorothy Hoffman at Paws Prints Post whose celebration of the human-animal bond on the Internet is a heart song in itself; St. Anthony's Continuing Care Center in Rock Island, Illinois, for research access to their archives; Vincent and Margaret Gaddis, whose revelations in *The Strange World of Animals and Pets* were inspirational; Ginny Jean Brancato for sharing compassion and resources; Londos D'arrigo for indispensable support from start to finish; my son, Jesse Mundis, for spreading the word on the Web; and the scores of cyber-situated animal lovers worldwide who responded with an overwhelming outpouring of anecdotes and stories, which I only regret could not all be included.

My deep appreciation also to Jack Hanna; Nancy Rose; George DeFina and the students of the Reginald R. Bennett Elementary School; Donna McCrohan Rosenthal; Wit

Acknowledgments

Tuttel; the Clearwater Marine Aquarium; Suncoast Seabird Sanctuary; Nancy Young and Jim Sanford at the Knoxville Zoo; Gordon McGregor Reid, Pat Cade, Neil Ormond, Chris Vere, and everyone at the Chester Zoo; the Montana School for the Deaf and the Blind Foundation; Susan Phillips Cohen; Marshall Powers; Joanie Abraham; Teri Ronayne; Joan Duffin; Tasha Grosz; Marilou Corrigan; Jean Marie Diaz; Rene Hindriks; Gary Holowicki; Walt Quader; Kevin Murphy; Jen Goodman; Edgar Rosenberg; Sue Shorey; Anna and her horse Chelsea Bun's; Leona Grieve; Deborah Cuyle; Carolyn Price; Christine Code at Ferret Forum; Pam Greene at Ferret Central; Phyllis Lindberg; Allen Patenaude; Mary Helen McMahon; Maggie Polk; the Glen Cove Lions Club; Anne Burnett; Susan Yecies; Linda Spear; Denice Ciccio; Susan and Shep Siegel; Karen Kelly; Ken Winston Caine; and Milly Marmur, without whom these heart songs would never have been sung.

Foreword
By Jack Hanna

There is a bond between humans and animals that is as undeniable and immeasurable as the amount of love a heart can hold. Anyone who has known the joy of an animal's lifetime companionship, or even just shared its world for a short while, has been fortunate. I have been more than fortunate; I have been privileged. Animals are not just part of my life, they *are* my life.

When I was five years old growing up on our farm in Tennessee, my first pets were a couple of collies. These animals were, for me, the fauna equivalent of peanuts—I couldn't stop with just two. Before long my pet posse included pigs, goats, horses, rabbits, birds, and even a groundhog. And I was crazy about all of them. At one point my rabbit collection multiplied to more than 100, but rather than part with a single one (no pet of mine was going to wind up as stew), I let every last cotton-tailed one of those hoppers loose. And as more and more wonderfully incredible animals entered my life, the more wonderfully incredible I realized these creatures were.

The full depth and breadth of the human-animal relationship hit home when, at the age of two, our daughter Julie was diagnosed with leukemia. Due to her lack of immunity, she developed pneumonia and a potentially deadly staph infection. She was rushed to a hospital in Memphis and immediately placed in a sterile intensive-care unit where she spent the next two months in isolation to protect her from infectious disease. It was a long, slow ordeal for everyone—especially Julie—who had to endure years of chemotherapy, radiation, bone-marrow transplants, and spinal taps to beat the odds against her. But, incredibly, she did. And what's even more incredible is that there's no doubt in any of our minds that her pet bunny, Flopsy, helped her do it. As vital as all the medical procedures were, it was Julie's bond with animals, especially Flopsy, that through this seemingly endless painful period provided her with the indomitable will to get well. Since then, I have never questioned the healing wonders of animals—nor will readers of this worldwide gathering of heart songs, a laughter and tears collection of personal testaments to the many facets of our marvelous human-animal bond.

If there is one thing that I've learned from all my adventures meeting and interacting with different species around the globe it's that everyone enjoys a good animal story. I have also discovered that there is a particular breed with an unquenchable desire for telling and listening to these stories. We are called Animal Lovers.

Hester Mundis, whom I came to know while working on my *Ultimate Guide to Pets*, is a permanent pressed-to-the-heart animal lover. Over the years, her personal ark has embraced dogs, cats, birds, iguanas, fish, and even a chimpanzee! In this book of true reminiscences from ordinary and extraordinary people, about ordinary and extraordinary animals, she has reached into that heartland we all share and put together a rich assortment of life stories *from* animal lovers *for* animal lovers. Yes, we are a special breed. And, as you'll find with every turn of a page, there is a special heart song for each of us.

—JACK HANNA

DIRECTOR EMERITUS, COLUMBUS ZOO WILDLIFE
CORRESPONDENT FOR *GOOD MORNING AMERICA*
HOST OF THE NATIONALLY SYNDICATED
JACK HANNA'S ANIMAL ADVENTURES

Contents

Introduction

The first motion picture my parents ever took me to see was *Lassie Come Home*. I was only about five at the time and unaware that such things as "Hollywood Endings" existed. To my mind, a seemingly insoluble solution—like one where a beloved dog is badly hurt, starving, lost, and hundreds of miles from her home—was, well, obviously *insoluble*. I sobbed so loudly that people beseeched my parents to take me out of the theater, but I refused to leave. (It seemed like deserting an animal in need.) When Lassie finally did come home, I bawled even louder than when she was en route. After that, I desperately wanted a dog so that I could make up for all the hardships that Lassie had endured. (I was a very metaphysical five-year-old.)

Every afternoon for months afterward when my mother would come home from shopping, I'd look up from my piano practice and say, "Did you bring me a dog?" She'd just shake her head, and I'd go back to "Für Elise." After two years of asking the same question and still not mastering "Für Elise," I finally got my dog. She was part beagle, part spitz; low-slung and high-spirited. I named her after Lassie; I called her Pal. I'd read somewhere that Pal was Lassie's *real* name. It was as close to Lassie verisimilitude as I was going to get with a beagle-spitz mix.

Pal was my dog for 13 years. I can still remember the feel

of her sleek white-and-black coat, her cool nose, and the way her tail used to swat my legs when I came home from school. There were many years growing up when I was convinced that she was the only one in the world who understood me—and she probably was.

When I was 11, I wanted a horse. I was at that "National Velvet" stage. My family had a small nonworking farm in New Jersey where we used to spend our summers. One morning, my father told me that there was a *surprise* for me in the barn. My heart thumped for joy.

"Your surprise has four legs," he said, "and hoofs."

I was ecstatic.

"And," he added, "she has horns."

Horns? That was a surprise all right.

Her name was Sweetie Pie. She was a pure-white goat, with a wispy goatee, and a nose that was made for nuzzling. We got her to pull a cart, but that's about as horselike as she ever got. She much preferred to think of herself as a dog, following us into the house and climbing up and down the stairs. I swear she would have chased sticks if she could have caught them.

From then on, there were always animals in my life. All of them enriched it—and some, like Boris the chimpanzee I raised for nearly three years in a Manhattan apartment, changed it forever.

People talk about their animals the way parents talk about their children. The difference is it's a lot more fun to hear about their animals. I've always loved these stories. They're outrageously biased, unabashedly emotional, and conveyed with such an honest lack of self-consciousness that a wonderful sort of osmosis occurs upon hearing them. From animal lover to animal lover, they affirm an unspoken kinship and cut straight to your heart. The ones you'll find in this book are here for just that reason.

Love at First Sight

"One does not meet oneself until one catches the reflection from an eye other than human."

LOREN EISELEY, AMERICAN ANTHROPOLOGIST

RATIONALITY, LOGIC, AND COMMON SENSE DON'T ENTER THE PICTURE WHEN YOU LOSE YOUR HEART TO A BABY CHIMPANZEE.

A Joyous Insanity

When I first saw Boris, he was lying on a blanket of shredded newspaper in a kitten carrying case in a not-so-reputable New York pet shop—a helpless, frightened, and unbelievably adorable orphan baby chimpanzee. Dark chocolate eyes were set in a light mocha face that was as soft as doeskin, and on his chin was a powder-white fuzz of a beard. His hair was silky and black and parted in the center of his head, bristling out at the sides around two outrageously comic big ears. Something this cute, I thought, could not be real. It was undoubtedly a very ingenious battery-operated toy. Somewhere on his underside there had to be a tag that said, "Made in Japan." But suddenly I was holding him, and there was no tag in sight. In one magic moment, he threw his arms around my neck, thoroughly wet my coat, and, though I did not know it then, totally annihilated a lifetime of rationality and logic.

Common sense didn't enter the picture. He needed a mom. I was already a working mother with an eight-year-old son and couldn't see what difference a chimp would make in our lives—and neither did my husband, Jerry. Boy, did we have a lot to learn! Boris changed all our lives completely and forever.

We raised him in our Manhattan apartment, along with our rambunctious German shepherd, Ahab, for nearly three years, learning the hard though often hilarious way that what is okay behavior in the jungle can be a disaster in an apartment—especially where the closest things to vines are drapes, pole lamps look like trees, and your prime playmate is the most-feared dog in the neighborhood. (Boris's early years were an expensive proposition, too. Aside from the 750 pounds of bananas he ate annually, antique vases that had come through the Revolution unscathed didn't survive 15 minutes with Boris.) But it wasn't until I discovered that I was expecting another baby that we realized Boris needed—and deserved—a permanent home of his own, with his own.

We researched all the zoos in the world (literally), and Chester Zoo in England was like an answer to our prayers. Not only had numerous animal authorities lauded it for its excellence, especially in its treatment of apes (who could romp and play on an island without bars), but the zoo's founder, Mr. Mottershead, assured us that Boris would never be given away for research and would have a home at Chester for life.

Boris knew something was amiss, and in the weeks and days before his departure he repeatedly tried to bring things back to normal, which scored us all the more. Whenever one of us would pet him lovingly, wistfully, in that poignantly brave but transparently sad way indicative of goodbyes, he would pull away and try to strike up a game or a chase. Sometimes he'd crawl up on my lap and roll over on his back, begging to be tickled. I'd force myself to giggle and laugh with him as I had in the past, but it fooled neither of us. I found myself encouraging him and Ahab in relay games. At least Ahab could play with him for extended periods without crying.

We made arrangements with BOAC (the British Overseas Airlines Corporation) to fly Boris to Manchester and bought a small, sturdy carrying case to ship him in. Although tranquilizers are often given to animals being shipped by air, we were advised against it. We changed Boris's flight to one that coincided with his bedtime and confirmed with Chester that someone from the zoo would be at the airport to meet him the following morning.

The day of Boris's departure arrived, as we'd known it would. I dressed him in his red and white polo shirt. He was excited and happy knowing that he was going out, which only tore more at my heart. The cab ride to Kennedy Airport was excruciatingly painful. Boris was loving every minute of peering out the window, and the taxi driver kept asking us why we were crying. It hurt too much to explain.

At the terminal, we prepared Boris's carrying case for the flight. We took a newspaper and shredded it, just as we had when we first brought him home from the pet store. We put it in the case along with some lettuce, apple slices, and a piece of my sweatshirt, which he'd always cuddled at night as a sort of security blanket. Then I undressed him and put him inside. Jerry grabbed my hand, and we kissed Boris goodbye. I couldn't stop the tears.

The next morning, we received a cable from the zoo telling us that Boris had arrived "safe, happy, and neatly packed." A week later we got a long, newsy letter from Mr. Mottershead telling us that Boris not only was doing well but was a hit with all the visitors, cutting up with antics and reveling in his increased audiences.

Photographs followed, and we were pleased to see that Boris's new friends looked like just the sort we wanted him to hang out with. As heart-wrenching a decision as it was to part with our little fluff ball, as we called him, he is happy at Chester.

In the 27 years that he has been there, Boris has thrived with the companionship of his own kind (he is now the proud father of 12) and basked in the attentive care of his keepers (one of whom, Neil Ormond, has been there since the day he arrived). Somehow, in his own special way, he's managed to bridge the evolutionary gap that separates men from apes—enjoying the rest of his days in the best of all alien worlds.

I visited him twice in the first 12 years he was there, each time bringing him his favorite foods (tiny marshmallows, raisins, and a chocolate Yoo-Hoo drink). He'd hoot, I'd cry, and partings were always difficult. It was May when I made my third visit; it had been 15 years since last I saw him.

Boris looked handsomer than ever! I realized that 15 years was a long time between visits and a lot had happened in both our lives, so once again I'd brought his favorite raisins and marshmallows to spark memories that could help him remember our connection.

At first it looked as if his only interest was in the food. But as I called out to him, using phrases he once knew, such as "What do you think of that?" and "Give me a kiss!" his attention became more focused on me. He hooted several times. I used to know what every one of his grunts and hoots meant when he was a baby, but this time I wasn't sure. (Indeed his voice had grown a lot deeper.) But when he went inside the chimp house, he stared at me through the glass.

For a long moment, we held each other with our eyes— mine, of course, filling with tears—and in his gaze there was a glint of recognition, a perception of something special between us. He might not have remembered me as his "mom," but he remembered something—and that meant everything to me. As we were walking away, I turned for one last look back. Now, I might have imagined it—or it might have been the tears in my eyes—but his arm was outstretched, and I could have sworn he blew me a kiss goodbye.

—HESTER MUNDIS

Today Boris is the dominant chimp at the Chester Zoo and a favorite with visitors. His likeness appears on souvenir chocolate coins sold at the gift shop, which makes me smile. For me, he's always been what sweet dreams were made of.

WHEN YOU FALL IN LOVE WITH
AN ANIMAL THAT DOESN'T REALLY
BELONG TO YOU, YOU MAY DO A
LOT OF THINGS YOU WOULDN'T EXPECT
YOU'D DO TO MAKE IT YOURS.

The Buyback Pup

It was in September 1989 when our little Boston terrier BooBoo gave birth to her first litter. My husband, Steve, and I had been planning for weeks, preparing a whelping box, making Boo comfortable, and taking deposits on the expected pups. As the day drew near, I began taking her temperature. We were told it would drop two degrees or more several hours before she went into labor, and Steve and I wanted to be prepared. It was our first litter, too.

Early Sunday morning, Boo's labor began. I don't know who was more nervous—her or us. Finally, the first pup arrived. Not quite sure what to do, Boo took it in her mouth and began to shake it. She seemed confused by the tiny thing, though in a matter of minutes instinct took over, and she proved to be the great mom we knew she would be, delivering four more pups and gently caring for them.

A few days later, I noticed that the first pup seemed to have a strange odor. I picked him up and found that he had a small tear on his stomach, and it appeared to be infected. We called the vet immediately and made arrangements to bring the little guy in. It turned out that when Boo had shaken the pup at birth, she'd ripped the umbilical cord from his body, leaving a small open wound that had begun to fester. But whether it was simply a muscle tear or a deeper more serious wound was now the question. Since the pup was only two days old and quite small, the vet suggested that it might be best to put the little fella down.

I looked at my six-foot, 250-pound husband holding this little nine-ounce bundle in one hand, his eyes filling up with tears, and knew what the answer would be. "No way!" We told her to do whatever it takes. "Just fix him!"

We took the pup home so that he could nurse and awaited the vet's call to say that she was ready and we could bring him back in as soon as possible. As I watched him eat, I thought of a passage from *The Living Bible* in Matthew, chapter 7, verses 7–11: "Ask, and you will be given what you ask for." So, I prayed to St. Matthew to protect this tiny puppy and, in so doing, named him Matthew.

It turned out that Matthew only needed four stitches to close up the tear and was going to be just fine! He remained the runt of the litter, with a really laid-back personality. And within five weeks, he had become Steve's little buddy, sleeping beside him between our pillows, following him around the yard, climbing into his lap to watch TV.

At seven weeks, the pups were ready to go to their new homes. One by one we watched them go. All but Matt. The woman who had chosen him phoned and asked if we could keep him until Christmas Eve because he was to be a gift for her husband. Of course, we said yes.

As December 24 drew closer, Steve and I both knew there was no way were going to be able to give Matthew up, but we also knew that he belonged to someone else. What we didn't know was what we were going to do about it.

Christmas Eve arrived. I had arranged to meet the woman at the shopping mall where I worked since it was halfway between our houses. Steve left for work that morning almost in tears. "Please try and talk her into letting us keep Matt," he said. I told him I'd try. But I didn't have a plan. We had taken a deposit, given our word, and now our hearts were breaking. It didn't feel like Christmas Eve at all. What we needed was something like a miracle. And just then I had idea, which, as it turned out, was close enough.

There was a pet shop in the mall that sold puppies, and a friend of mine worked there. My plan was simple: I would tell the woman who was buying Matthew exactly what the problem was, that we had fallen in love with Matt and, if she was willing, I would not only return her $100 deposit but give her an additional $100. With this money—and the

$400 that she still owed us—she would be able to purchase any puppy at the pet shop! I would simply buy back my precious Matthew.

The woman was reluctant, especially after seeing Matthew, but she finally agreed to at least look at the ones in the store. My friend showed her all the puppies, one after another, and the woman played with each of them in turn, as well as with Matthew, then repeated the process. Finally, after 2½ hours (it seemed an eternity), she had narrowed her selection down to a little white Highland terrier and Matthew. I waited and prayed.

First, she looked as if she were going for Matt—then, suddenly (something like another miracle) she said, "No, I've always wanted a white dog, and this one seems really happy. I'll take him."

As my friend took care of sending her home with her new puppy, Matthew and I made a quick getaway before she could change her mind. Once we were safely home, Matt looked at me as if to say, "Mom, let's go for another ride. That was fun." *Fun?* If he only knew! Steve returned from work an hour later. The look on his face when Matthew came running out of the room to greet his "Dad" was the very best Christmas present I could ever have gotten. From that day on, Sir Matthew Scooter—the very best Christmas present *we* could have gotten—became a part of our lives forever!

Our beloved Matthew is now nine years old and a dad himself. Scooter's Princess Bristol, born July 19, 1997, is very much her father's daughter—with a lively little bit of devil mixed in. Sadly, Boo passed away two months before the birth of her granddaughter. But her gentle, loving spirit lives on in Matthew, her special firstborn son who will always be our special firstborn, too.

—PATTY MUDGE

♥

"All animals are equal, but some animals are more equal than others."

GEORGE ORWELL, BRITISH AUTHOR

WHEN A LITTLE CRITTER WITH A LOT OF
HEART FINDS YOU, YOU'RE HIS FOR LIFE.

Mylo and Me

Mylo was my first ferret. I'd gone into a pet store to pass time while my sister had her braces tightened. I was playing with the ferrets that were there and happened to pick up Mylo. Well, he looked up at me as if to say, "It's about time!" and immediately curled himself in my arms and fell asleep.

I never put him down. I paid for him and a cage and left the store. I didn't put him down until I got in the car. Even then, he insisted on curling up on my lap to sleep.

That night, and every night for the first six months of his life, Mylo slept with me. Wherever I was, he had to be. I'd let him hide in my jacket when I went to the store. When he had to stay home so I could go to school, he'd wait patiently in his cage until I returned—then, of course, he'd demand to be let out. No matter what my mood, he could put a smile on my face and make me believe it belonged there. Being with him was the best part of my day—even when his idea of helping me with an important homework assignment was stealing my highlighters and hiding them under the dresser—and it still is!

Mylo now has Lacy, my other ferret, to play with. But the one-on-one time we've shared since the day he chose me at that pet shop has convinced me that some of the smallest animals have the biggest hearts. A lot of large, two-legged animals could learn a lot about love from a critter like Mylo.

—SUMMER RANKIN

"There is no language barrier between people and the animals that love them."

HEART SONG

SHE WAS A DOG WHO NEVER KNEW LOVE
AND NEVER KNEW FREEDOM. IT SEEMED AS
IF SHE HAD TO CHOOSE BETWEEN THEM—
UNTIL SHE RECOGNIZED A SPECIAL HUMAN
HEART.

Sophie's Choice

Rocky had been gone three years, and I felt it was time
for another dog. Our local SPCA (Society for the Prevention
of Cruelty to Animals) needed volunteers for walking dogs,
so I thought that would be a good way to become acquainted
and find one that was right for me. (After all, I had *some* re-
quirements: not a barker, not too hyper, and, well, kind of
looked like Rocky.)

I was overwhelmed by the noise and odor at the shelter
and heartbroken at the sight of all the homeless animals. For
three hours, I walked (was pulled by) puppies, feisty shepherds, determined Dalmatians, and far too many pit bulls. I
felt I was doing a good deed, but I wasn't making a connection. This was going to take longer than I thought.

As I was leaving for the day, a staff member asked if I'd been to "the garage." He explained that was where they kept animals in quarantine, and at the moment they had quite a few there. It seemed that when a local woman had been arrested for murder, the police had found 20 dogs and a dozen miniature horses all filthy, malnourished, and locked together in her basement.

I followed the staffer to the garage where all 20 dogs were being kept. They had been there for three months and were now ready for adoption. The moment we entered, my heart started to pound. It wasn't because of the way the dogs lunged at their crate doors or cried and barked and smelled, it was because they all looked like Rocky! Scruffy Benji-types, somewhere between adorable terrier and lovable sheepdog. Just what I was looking for!

After composing (and pinching) myself, I noticed that only one of these dogs was not barking. She was crouched in the corner of her crate, sort of trying to be invisible. I could relate. More than that, I knew I wanted to.

It took two husky guys 15 minutes to get a leash on her. None of the dogs had ever been out of that woman's basement, let alone on leashes. I began to have second thoughts, but only for a second. What was I getting into? Who knew? Who cared? It was love at first sight—at least on my part—and that was that. Or was it?

I christened the dog Sophia-Love, which I figured she needed a lot of, and called her Sophie. I should have named her Pacer because that's what she did, pace back and forth.

She'd come to me and then withdraw as soon as I put my hand out. But I could deal with that. I could also have named her Phewey because that's how she smelled (Eau de Kennel #5!). But I could deal with that, too. But, and this was a big but, if nothing else my dog had to be a car dog. Happily, right from the start, Sophie was! I'd take the top off my Jeep, and we both let our hair blow in the wind. She loved it. I swear that every time she was in that car, she looked like she was laughing.

Sophie's debut into people society was at a friend's barbecue one early summer evening. She was adjusting pretty quickly although I always kept a leash on her. It was a red, rather heavy leash meant for a large dog, but I felt comfortable with it on Sophie as she was unusually strong for her size.

After dinner, my friend Mel and I took Sophie for a walk to a nearby stream still swollen from spring rains. The noise of the water crashing against the rocks was almost deafening. I was anxious to see Sophie's reaction. To my surprise and delight, she wasn't frightened in the least. In fact, she didn't hesitate to wade in the shoals. I thought again about bathing her. She still had an obnoxiously strong kennel odor, but I had been advised to hold off on a bath until she became more comfortable with her new environment. I decided not to risk it.

As the last light of evening was fading, we headed back up the path for home. Mel and I were engaged in an animated discussion when suddenly Sophie gave a sharp tug, and I dropped the leash. For a brief moment our eyes met. I saw it instantly: two years old and never having anything close to freedom, not being with me long enough to establish trust. She was gone in a flash, her red leash trailing behind her. It was all uphill, and she had the advantage. The last I saw of her was as she disappeared behind Mel's house into the woods. It was almost dark; there were no other houses close by. I knew we could do nothing more until morning.

As soon as it was light, Mel and I split up in different directions, combing the surrounding Catskill woods. I figured we'd find her in a few hours. After all, she was dragging a heavy leash and was sure to get caught on something. I hadn't realized the remoteness of the area. All driveways dead-ended at the mountain's edge, after which there was nothing but wild, undeveloped forest. No Sophie in sight.

By noon we had alerted all the local residents to be on the lookout for her. I put up signs around the area and in town. I notified the authorities. I called a local dog trainer who did tracking. He brought three big Rottweilers to try to pick up her scent in the woods. They returned several hours later. No Sophie. I was sick with worry.

I spent every day that week hiking through the mountains in the area, and with each day realized more and more what an impossible and futile task it was. Finally, I forced myself to accept the fact that she was gone.

The following week, the skies opened up. We'd had a long spell of dry, hot weather, and now that was over. All of a sudden there was an avalanche of thunder, lightning, torrential rain, and hail. I hoped that the weeks before were Sophie's happiest—freedom as she never knew existed. I truly felt it was her choice to run. I consoled myself thinking that now she would be in doggie heaven and would always run free.

It was early July, a full moon, my birthday. The Big One! Older, yes—wiser? I hoped so. I was contemplating a lot of things when the phone rang. It was a neighbor of Mel's saying he'd found my dog; well, at least seen her. I didn't know if I should let myself believe it. He assured me that it was Sophie. She was dragging a red leash that had gotten wound up in brambles. He'd heard her bark, but when he approached her, she growled.

He gave me directions. Follow the streambed two miles up to where it makes a sharp curve left. Stay on a sort of path till it hits the stream again and go another mile. Look for an abandoned house, half-fallen-down. "That's where she is," he said.

Right. Piece of cake! Luckily, Sophie heard (or sensed) me stumbling through the woods and barked. I followed that welcome sound, and finally there she was—snarled in brush, red leash dangling, and, to my amazement, tail wagging. How she survived those weeks I'll never know. And she'll never know how grateful I was that she did. When we got home, she was ravenously hungry and still scruffy and scared. But she was clean! She smelled like a daisy. All those days in the rain served to clean her right up. It was a great birthday present. A milestone birthday present. So much so that we now celebrate our birthdays together every year—with a bottle of champagne (for me), a bowl of Milk-Bones (for her), and a bubble bath for both of us!

—CAROLANN BERNIUS

❧

"The great pleasure of a dog is that you may make a fool of yourself with him and not only will he not scold you, but he will make a fool of himself, too."

SAMUEL BUTLER, ENGLISH AUTHOR

Dog Wagging Tale

Late last summer, I accompanied my friend Mary to a grungy garage on Manhattan's Lower East Side to get an insurance inspection photo for her brand-new used car. As soon as we got to the place, we were aware of the dogs: a group of pit bull mixes as grungy as their surroundings. One of them, an apparent American Staffordshire/boxer mix that looked like a shrunken Rhodesian Ridgeback because she was so emaciated, walked tentatively toward us. I reached down to pet her, and it seemed to be just what she'd wanted. She twitched her hindquarters and kind of wiggled against me. She was really sweet, so sweet I didn't mind that the layer of grime from her never-washed coat quickly coated my hand.

Suddenly, a burly man entered the garage and for no reason at all started nastily jabbing an umbrella at the dog. Amazingly, she didn't cower or retreat. Instead, she sat down on my feet, as if to protect *me* from this person, and began barking vociferously. The man then grabbed a wooden scrub brush from a shelf and—to my horror—whacked the dog hard on her head. Thinking quickly, I screamed, "Stop! Why are you beating my dog?"

"Your dog? Ha!" The man laughed and smugly identified himself as one of the mechanics that worked there. My bluff had failed miserably.

Neither Mary nor I had (thankfully) ever witnessed such outright animal cruelty firsthand. In what we now call our "Black Beauty" moment, Mary offered to buy the dog for $50. The mechanic snorted and told us that the dog's role was that of a guard and that she was going to stay right where she was. (He meant the garage, though where she actually *was* at that moment was right by my feet.) Then he gave her another smack to the head and walked away.

When he was gone, another mechanic from the garage who had overheard the exchange approached us. Looking around to make sure we were alone, he asked if we would give the dog a good home. When we said we would give her the best, he told us to do just that. He refused any payment; his only request was that we give her a bath. We did that first thing!

Three baths later, her coat was shining. Of course, being a dog, the first thing she wanted to do was cavort through our garden and get covered in dirt again. But earth was a far preferable cover to the grime and grease that had blanketed her skin since birth.

When we took her to the vet for shots and spaying the

next day, we discovered that the tales about a pit bull's evil temperament were propaganda. Prior to the exam, the vet had asked us if he needed to use a muzzle on the dog. We said yes because she was new to us and we didn't really know how she would react. About 30 seconds into the examination, the vet removed the restraint. He told us he could already sense that this was a dog with no need of a muzzle.

Her temperament has only improved in the months since we found her, or more accurately, since she found us, and the joy in her new life is matched only by ours in sharing it. We named her Betty Boop, after a Betty Boop figurine that dangled from Mary's brand-new used-car keys that day at the garage. The only other legacy of Betty's early days seems to be her desire to sleep under a bed; at the garage, the only safe place where she could avoid being hit was under a car. Although she may always feel more secure with a ceiling very close to her back, I think she knows that everywhere is a safe haven for her now—and will be so for many years to come.

—MARY ELLEN KENNEL

❧

"I think I could turn and live with animals,
they are so placid and self-contained . . . They do
not sweat and whine about their condition."

WALT WHITMAN, AMERICAN POET

Voices

"How could you not fall in love with a sheep that thought it was a dog?"

TOM KIZIS

❧

"We bought him as a watchdog, but he's hopeless. He'd lick a burglar to death."

JEANNIE MACKEY

❧

"Our cat learned to open the fridge. It had the timing so perfect, it would hit its paw against the seal and then jump onto the bench, into the fridge and eat the food—Glad wrap and all! So we got a new refrigerator. Within a week, she had that worked out, too."

HELEN KIMMET

"I'd rather kiss my cat good night than my grandpa. My cat's whiskers are softer."

KATRINA FREER

"You know what we call people who say that they're 'just going to look at the puppies?' Dog owners."

SHARON ROTHE

"Our cat Lulu opens all our closet doors. She doesn't go into the closets, she just likes the doors to be open. She comes from England, so maybe it's a British thing."

AMY FRIEDMAN

Devoted to You

"The one, absolute, unselfish friend that man can have in this selfish world, the one that never deserts him, the one that never proves ungrateful or treacherous, is his dog."

SENATOR GEORGE GRAHAM VEST

HE WAS A DOG WHOSE LOYALTY AND
FAITHFULNESS TO ONE MAN WAS THE ONLY
WORLD HE KNEW—OR EVER WANTED.

The Vigil

On August 24, 1924, Francis McMahon of Erie, Illinois, was planning to fix some window frames around his home. His dog, Shep, a gold-and-russet Scotch collie, happily trailed his master as he went about gathering the materials he needed. The dog knew that after work was done, there would be a long walk through the field, maybe even some stick throwing. They always had good times when they went out together. His master had just started down the stairs to the basement, when suddenly he lost his footing and fell headlong to the cement floor below, where he lay motionless.

Shep licked McMahon's face, whined, but when his master did not move, the dog began to bark nonstop. The incessant barking alerted neighbors who found the unconscious McMahon and immediately rushed him to the hospital. Shep would not leave his master's side.

By the time they arrived at St. Anthony's Hospital in

Rock Island, McMahon, who was suffering from a fractured skull, had come to. As the stretcher was being wheeled to an elevator, Shep tried to follow.

McMahon patted the dog's head affectionately. "It's all right. We'll walk the field later." Giving him a final pat, he said, "Be a good dog; wait for me here."

Shep had heard the words before, he knew they meant he was to stay where he was until his master returned. He lay down and watched the elevator doors shut. He closed his eyes. They'd walk the field later.

The next day, Francis McMahon died, and his body was taken from the hospital by another exit. Shep stayed in the lobby in a spot where he could keep a constant eye on the elevator. Each time the elevator descended, Shep would rush forward, tail wagging, waiting by the doors, only to return again to his place. He'd wait. He was a good dog.

McMahon's family tried to get Shep to come home with them, but the dog refused. The Franciscan Sisters at St. Anthony's gave him food and water, but for a long while Shep would not eat. Day and night, he maintained his lonely vigil on the first floor of the hospital, never leaving for more than 15 minutes at a time—always listening for the sound of the elevator so that he would be there when the doors opened and his master returned. He was a good dog; he'd been told to wait.

The days turned into weeks and the weeks turned into years, and still Shep awaited his master's return. Eventually, the Franciscan Sisters who ran St. Anthony's "adopted" him, giving him regular meals and a soft mat to lie on, but his loyalty was to his master. He made friends with some of the sisters and nurses but remained aloof with all but a select few.

As the years passed, his loyalty and faithfulness became widely known and admired by thousands of people who learned his story. And along with stories of his unflinching devotion and tireless vigil, other tales began to circulate, tales of an uncanny sense possessed by Shep.

Hospital staff reported that in the dead hours of the night, Shep would suddenly spring up from a nap, rush toward the silent elevator, wag his tail, and emit a joyful little bark. For a moment, ears perked, his eyes would brighten. Then, disappointed once more, he'd slink back to his corner.

There were rumors that two of the sisters once heard the sound of an elevator when it was motionless; another sister was said to have seen a bluish light beside the dog. Dog experts explained that canines often have a strange psychic sense not shared by humans, though they conceded that an animal sustained by such unshakable belief might simply be dreaming the realization of his lifelong wish.

Shep's vigil came to an end on a foggy night in December of 1936. Old, with failing eyesight and limited mobility, he had gone for a short trip to the curb outside the hospital. The driver of the truck never saw him. Shep was killed instantly. After almost $12\frac{1}{2}$ years, his faith in being reunited with his master was finally rewarded. They would walk the fields of heaven together, forever.

On April 6, 1937, the American Humane Association

memorialized Shep with a beautiful bronze plaque that was hung in the lobby of St. Anthony's Hospital (now OSF St. Anthony's Continuing Care Center). The inscription reads:

In Fond Memory of
Shep
A Gallant Collie
Who Followed His Mortally Injured Master
Into This Hospital in 1924 and Remained True
To His Orders "Wait Here" Until His Own Accidental
Death in December 1936
This Faithful Dog Shall Bear Him Company

—HESTER MUNDIS

SOMETIMES WHEN A DOG DOESN'T DO
WHAT IT'S TOLD, IT'S BECAUSE IT IS
LISTENING WITH ITS HEART.

Patience Rewarded

Albert Payson Terhune, the famed dog writer of the 1920s and 1930s, often told the story of how his friend Wilson came to learn that what seems to be in the best interest of all concerned may not apply when one of those concerned is a dog.

Wilson's dog, Jack, was an energetic six-year-old collie that would meet him every day at the trolley station when he returned from work. This was a ritual that had begun when Jack was a pup. The dog knew the route to and from the station like the back of his paw—and following that route was the highlight of his day. So, when Wilson changed jobs and had to move to California, he thought it best to leave Jack on his home turf in Philadelphia with a relative. He explained all this to the dog upon leaving and told him that they both would have to adjust to new homes.

But Jack, who had always listened to his owner, didn't

want a new home. He would not stay with the family he'd been left with. He returned to Wilson's old house, even though it was boarded up, and there he passed his solitary days beside an abandoned chair beneath the portico. But every evening, tail wagging, he trotted off to the trolley station. For as long as Jack had been in the world, Wilson had always taken the same trolley home from work, and Jack would be there to greet him. But evening after evening, there was no sign of the devoted dog's master. Confused and sad, he would return alone to the deserted house.

The dog's depression grew. He refused food and, as the days passed, he became thinner and thinner, his ribs becoming noticeable even through his thick blond coat. But every evening, ever hopeful, he'd go to the station to meet the trolley. And every evening, he'd return to the porch more despondent than before.

Jack's deteriorating condition did not go unnoticed. A friend who lived nearby was so upset by it that he took it upon himself to send a telegram to Wilson in California, informing him of the dog's situation.

That was all it took.

Wilson bought a return train ticket immediately; he knew what he had to do. Upon arriving in Philadelphia, he waited several hours just so that he could take the same trolley that he always did when coming home. When it arrived at the station, sure enough, there was Jack, waiting and watching as the passengers got off. Looking and hoping. And then suddenly there *he* was, his beloved owner. His master had returned at last! Jack's world was whole once more—and so was Wilson's.

"Jack was sobbing almost like a child might sob. He was shivering all over as if he had a chill. And I? Well, I blew my nose and did a lot of fast winking," Wilson later told Terhune, according to Vincent and Margaret Gaddis's account of the reunion in *The Strange World of Animals and Pets*.

Wilson took his devoted dog Jack back to California with him. They were never separated again.

—HESTER MUNDIS

❧

"The fidelity of a dog is a precious gift."

KONRAD Z. LORENZ, AUSTRIAN NATURALIST

WHEN A DOG MEANS EVERYTHING TO YOU,
CHANCES ARE YOU MEAN EVERYTHING TO
HIM, TOO.

Murphy

He came to me when he was two months old. A good friend knew that I had been thinking of getting a dog. So one day at work she made a phone call, and 10 minutes later a puppy was placed in my arms—it was love at first sight! I named him Murphy.

Murphy was very small when I got him. He was mostly white with a black-and-brown masked face, and he had three large black spots on his body. I used to call him my little speckled pup.

Murphy and I were together 10 years. I have never been married and have no other children (human or otherwise), so he was everything to me. He was there to laugh with me during the good times (he could really smile) and was there to console me during the bad. There was one point in my life when I had orthopedic surgery that went bad, and I almost lost my foot. For five long months, I was dependent on crutches and had to sleep on the couch. Murphy seemed to understand and know just what to do. He would always "ask" before he jumped up to lie next to me. And though he loved to go out frequently, when he realized that it was hard for me to get to the door, he held back and waited. He would sleep on the couch with me every night. But when my foot hurt and I'd ask him to get down, he would lie, uncomplaining, on the floor beside me. I kept a journal during this hard time, and as I read through it, I see that I wrote—over and over again—"Thank God for Murphy; I don't know what I would ever do without him."

We moved several times, and as hard as it was for me every time, Murphy was always there to be my friend when I didn't have any. We'd chase each other around the house, play tug, and go for long walks. When the men in my life left, there Murphy was, licking my ear and letting me know that he still loved me and that everything would be fine because he was there. I would talk to him constantly, tell him whatever I was thinking or feeling, and he would listen to my every word. I knew he understood. And just knowing that Murphy was always there for me with his unconditional love was enough to get me through anything.

He had so much character. I loved his different expressions, especially the quizzical way he cocked his head and looked at me with his beautiful brown eyes. And he had this big ol' grin that always made me smile. It wasn't your regular dog grin, it was an ear-to-ear people smile! I used to call him my little Pinocchio because I believed he wanted to be a real boy. If I had been gone for too long (to his way of thinking) or leaving again, man, would I get cussed out! He didn't bark; it was more of a jabbering thing. He'd snap his teeth together as if to say, "Hey, you're not spending enough time at home." I would always assure him that I'd be back later to play.

When I was home and Murphy got bored, he would go to a piece of furniture and scratch it with his paw, then he'd look at me and snap those darn teeth together. If I didn't pay any attention, he'd move on to another piece of furniture—from a chair, to the coffee table, to the stereo. He knew this made me angry and wouldn't quit until I paid attention to him.

Every time I put on my shoes, Murphy would bound to the door. When I'd tell him that he could come with me, he would nip at my feet all the way to the car as if to say, "Hurry up, let's go!" He loved to go anywhere with me. His collar now hangs on my rearview mirror so that he gets to go everywhere with me.

Over the years, Murphy had his share of ear infections and stitches, but, otherwise, he seemed healthy. Then one weekend that all changed. Without warning he had several "attacks" that caused him to hunch his back while sitting, pant frantically, and drool. I rushed him to the animal hospital.

On Monday morning, I found out that Murphy was full of cancer. It was so bad that they didn't even bother to remove any of it, and they couldn't tell me whether he would live a day or a month.

When I went to pick him up the following day, I was unsure of what I would see or what I would do. When the vet opened his cage, Murphy ran to the front door, scratched on it, and looked up at me as if to say, "Well, let's go home!" He seemed like his old self. I was suddenly filled with hope, but it was short-lived. After only a few hours, he was again in a lot of pain. I had heard that cancer patients sometimes get one more burst of energy before they go. I think Murphy knew how sick he was and wanted to be at home. But by that afternoon, I knew what I had to do. I kept saying to him, "You're going to make me do it today, aren't you?" It was his 10th birthday.

He was so very tired but would not sleep. He just sat there trying to keep himself propped up with his front legs, staring at me or out the window. It seemed that he was hanging on just for me—and *I* couldn't let go. I struggled with the thought of losing him but could not watch him suffer anymore. I called the vet. The vet was extremely nice and came to our house. It was done on our bed in "mama's loving arms." That's exactly what I told him as I carried him to his grave. He is now buried outside my bedroom window, the window he stared out of during his last hours. It's where I think he wanted to be.

As I look back, I wonder why I never knew he was that sick. Maybe the love we had between us was, in some way, a type of medicine. The cancer must have been there for a long time, but he never showed any signs of it. I don't know if he was hiding it from me, for me, but I guess I'll never know.

What I do know is that he will always be with me. A

few days after he died, I was walking down the hall, and I smelled him. I immediately cried because I knew he was there. I still "see" him walking up to me, wagging that stub tail of his, sticking his nose up so I will bend down and kiss him. As strange as this might sound (I have questioned my own sanity), I hear him in this little boy's voice, "Mama, I'm still here. I love you, I miss you, too." And when I go to sleep at night, I feel him curled up in the crook of my knees. It's funny, I still talk to him all the time and feel as if he hears me.

All the years we were together, I kept telling him, "Someday we'll have our very own house in the country." We moved to our new house in the country not quite two months before he died. I can't help but feel that Murphy waited for me to be happy and in a safe place before letting go. I still feel his presence and believe I always will. We were such a part of each other's lives that I don't think it could be any other way. I know for certain that I wouldn't want it to be.

"FOR MURPHY: BABY, MAMA WILL ALWAYS LOVE YOU,
FOREVER AND EVER, AMEN. YOU WILL
ALWAYS BE MY LITTLE BOY."

—ALISON PFAELZER

KATIE AND REBEL BELONGED TO EACH
OTHER FOR 10 YEARS. THEIR
CONVERSATIONS WERE PERSONAL; THEIR
LOVE FOR ONE ANOTHER UNQUESTIONED.

Rebel,
A Very Special Pony

We met him on a cold, crisp December day. His owner was a college student desperate to find a home for him before Christmas vacation ended, and my four-year-old daughter was equally desperate to have her own pony. When we saw him, he was standing in a field looking at us. At least from the glow in his eyes when he tossed his thick mane, you could surmise he was looking at us. Dad got on him bareback, with just a halter and lead rope, and cantered across the pasture without getting bucked off, so we figured he'd be okay for Katie. That's how Rebel came into our lives.

Looking like a Welsh pony but without papers to prove it, Rebel was a short, stocky, furry bay gelding. Although, when we got him home and turned him out with our small band of Arabian mares, he promptly rounded them up and stood guard over them. He took his position of protector very seriously, running off the dogs and even the people that attempted to come near. Rebel, alias "Studly Doolittle," put on such an act that even our stallion, looking on from his private paddock, was a little disturbed. Rebel was immediately dispatched to his own private paddock, where more-gelding-like manners gradually returned.

Of course, Katie was never put off by his antics. He was just living up to his name. She discovered, in short order, that he loved peanut-butter-and-jam sandwiches and Oreo cookies. He discovered equally quickly when lunchtime was, and he waited at his fence by the backyard for the little blonde-headed girl with half her lunch in her hands. They became fast friends.

That spring we took Rebel trail riding. Our family spent nearly all of our vacations riding in the mountains, so we had to see what sort of trail horse he would be. On our first outing at Silver Falls State Park near Stayton, Oregon, we let Katie and Rebel lead down the trail so we could keep an eye on them. It soon became apparent that this was not such a good idea. Rebel had a strong dislike for larger horses. So strong was his dislike that he wouldn't wait to get crowded to kick. No, he would run backward up the trail to get his licks in! Rebel and Katie were relegated to the back of the line.

Katie, though, was content back there. She could hold Rebel back and canter to catch up. Soon they were jumping logs and practicing leads and learning to post at the trot. Rebel would go anywhere. He'd march through the brush around the windfalls and wade through the creeks like a pro. He carried Katie everywhere in the Central Oregon Cascade Mountains and Wilderness areas; Tam McArthur Rim, Green Lakes, Park Meadow, Sister's Mirror Lake. He made Katie a trail rider.

One spring day, a couple of years later, a group of us went riding at Silver Falls. We stopped at a wide intersection, tied up the horses, and sat down in the grass for lunch. The horses were all content and standing quietly, or so we thought. All of a sudden, there stood Rebel, his halter hanging on the tree where he had rubbed it off. Katie was frantic, but I calmly informed her that he wasn't about to go anywhere and leave all of the other horses. Boy, was I wrong. All he was lacking was a mustache to twist. He gave us an evil smile, complete with a glint in his eye, then turned and bolted down the trail, tail up over his back.

One of our group, Sarah, quickly mounted her horse and took off after Rebel. Katie was in tears, fearful she would never see him again. And I must admit, as we sat and waited for what seemed like hours, I began to have my doubts. Well, Sarah caught him, but not without running him down and literally forcing him off the trail into bushes he couldn't run through. We never tied him again without putting the halter on so tight it nearly strangled him.

Katie also had showring dreams, and Rebel seemed to know his stuff, so we gave that a try. I cautioned Katie about keeping him away from big horses because he might kick. Secretly, I crossed my fingers and hoped she could keep him from backing up into other exhibitors. I needn't have worried. He got to the show, took one look around, and became "Rebel the Show Horse."

He tucked his head, with reins hanging below his knees, and marched into that ring like he owned it. I could tell early on that he was paying attention to every word the announcer said (probably from the whiplash Katie got when gait changes were called for). His transitions were perfect. He never missed a cue—from the announcer, that is—and Katie sat there, smiling broadly, collecting ribbons. By the time she was seven, she was an experienced exhibitor, with a wall full of blue ribbons and shelves full of trophies.

As years passed, we found ourselves a bit crowded in the barn. We considered putting Rebel in the same paddock as our stallion, Sam. Now, Sam was known to be a bit of a coward. During his own show career, his biggest problem was his lack of confidence when other horses crowded him. We weren't sure how he and Rebel would get along, but we thought we'd give it a try. Rebel promptly chased Sam out of his stall. Sam had never had to share his territory with anyone. He wasn't sure what to make of the little bay devil with the swishing tail and flattened ears. They had a delicate standoff for a while, then gradually Sam began to ask for his space back. Rebel acquiesced—to a point. They would share hay, but Sam got to keep his grain to himself. And when the weather was bad, they would *both* stand in the stall and watch it rain.

Rebel liked his new paddock. It was in front of the barn, bordering on both the driveway and the road. He soon learned Katie's bus schedule and would greet her daily with a whinny. She would reward him by saving her bread crusts and apple cores to feed him after school. On those occasional days when things weren't going right—a harsh word from me, an unfortunate comment by a friend at school—Katie would disappear to the barn with a handful of Oreos. The cookies were not for her. I don't know what she said to him; their conversations were very personal. I don't know what he said to her. All I know is when she came back to the house with cookie crumbs on her hands and horse "kisses" on her sleeves, she would be smiling and happy again.

For 10 years, Rebel and Katie belonged to each other. She developed confidence in rough backcountry and in showrings. While Rebel was still no angel and could cow-kick with the best of them, he was perfect with Katie. When no one else could make him move, she could pick up a canter from a standstill and change leads on the fly. On rainy afternoons when even Sam huddled in his stall, Rebel would wait up by the road for the bus and whinny when he saw it coming. Was it the apple cores and crusts of bread he waited for? I don't think so. I think it was Katie he wanted. And as for Katie, well, Rebel was just always there for her.

Old age is inevitable. It made its first impact on Rebel in the fall of 1989. Metabolic problems led to near-founder. His trail and show career ended but not his relationship to Katie. She looked after her old friend, hand-grazing him in the front yard, still taking her tears and smiles to share with him. I can't remember a morning he didn't whinny a greeting as she left for school or an afternoon he missed the arrival of her bus. She rode other horses on the trails and in the showrings, but Rebel still owned her heart.

Katie turned 14 this year. She is a long way from the 4-year-old with the long, golden pigtails flying down her back. This past year, she trained her own horse, a 3-year-old Arabian filly. As I watched her guide that youngster up the trail toward Green Lakes with tremendous confidence this summer, I thought about the first time she rode there on Rebel. As she calmly coaxed the 3-year-old over snowdrifts and across fast-flowing creeks, I silently thanked Rebel for all he had done. When she won her first blue ribbon on that frisky filly, I recalled that first blue Rebel had won for her. Was it luck we found him that December day? Or are some things just meant to be?

We said goodbye to Rebel on October 14, 1993. He will be missed.

—KAREN BRAG, AUTHOR OF *THE NATURE OF THE BEAST*

❧

"Some of my best leading men have been dogs or horses."

ELIZABETH TAYLOR, AMERICAN ACTRESS

Voices

"I don't think I could ever be poor enough not to feed my cats."

ANNEMARIE ZANCHETTI

❦

"One year I missed all the Christmas parties because I was home feeding our cat through a straw."

SUE WILENS

❦

"After our dog slipped, he became afraid to walk across our hardwood floors. They were really beautiful, but what could we do? We carpeted the house."

DENISE FUTTERMAN

❧

"People said, 'You're crazy for doing this.' I said, 'I just can't imagine not doing it.'"

SALLY PREWETT, on borrowing money for the $3,000 it cost to get a new kidney for her six-year-old cat, Bandit

❧

"He's a good boy. . . . He represents 12 years of my life; I've got to give him a chance."

LAURAN WALK, on spending several thousand dollars for hydrotherapy to treat her 12-year-old Shih Tzu, Sydnee, after his surgery for a ruptured disk

Healing Fur
and Feathers

*"Souls of animals infuse themselves
into the trunks of men."*

WILLIAM SHAKESPEARE, ENGLISH PLAYWRIGHT AND POET

THERE ARE CREATURES THAT ARE TRULY
ANGELS AMONG US—AND SOME EVEN COME
WITH THEIR OWN WINGS.

Ruby-Feathered Messenger

I got Ruby from a feed store. She was in a cage with a bunch of other chickens. I had a flock already, but I wanted another hen. When the owner asked me which one, I said, "Whichever one you can catch first."

So he gave me this chicken, and I took her home and put her in with the others. The next day, as I was throwing feed, she walked up to me and stood on my feet. And I thought, "Oh, great. He sold me a sick chicken."

I reached down and picked her up, and all of a sudden she started rubbing her head on my chin, softly clucking all sorts of chicken words. I think I knew right then that this was no ordinary chicken. She was a little Rhode Island Red, so I named her Ruby; she turned out to be a gem.

Ruby followed me around, would come when she was

called, and was the most amazingly social chicken I had ever known. I had been thinking for quite a while about using a bird for therapy, visiting seniors at nursing homes, but birds generally posed too many problems. We at the Delta Society do careful screening for animals that are involved in our visiting programs. I'd worked with dogs, cats, rabbits, a horse, and a donkey, but birds were tricky. Many of them have natural behaviors that can make them dangerous in therapy settings. (They climb and use their beaks as extra hands, which can be frightening to people who don't know birds.) Also, they tend to be unpredictable. But here was Ruby, a chicken—a domestic bird! She was just what I'd been looking for.

Ruby was the perfect candidate for therapy. I started by training her to wear a leash and a harness. She liked it. She liked people. She liked being petted by people. And it just kept getting better from there.

We've trained her to sit in a basket and stay. When she has to go—she tells you. She'll start clucking and wiggling (the signal is pretty clear), and then I'll take her out of the basket and put her somewhere appropriate so that she can relieve herself. I can give her a bath in the sink and then blow-dry her, and she just stands there and thinks it's fine.

Ruby has never pecked at anyone's glasses or jewelry, which is really unusual because chickens generally peck at shiny things. She "talks" softly and rubs her head against everyone I've ever handed her to. If she sits on someone's shoulder during a visit, she is very gentle about getting down when she's had enough. And if a child happens to squeeze her too hard, she just clucks a bit to let us know.

I use Ruby for numerous demonstration projects across the country. When she's away from the flock for any length of time, she has to work her way back up the chicken ladder when she returns, but she never seems to mind. If ever a bird was "unflappable," it's Ruby. She was once with me in Chicago at a conference where there were more than 50 dogs. Never fazed her. (She even reprimanded a golden retriever with a gentle nose peck when he got too curious.) When we appeared on the *Sally Jessy Raphaël Show* with a live audience and cameras all around, Ruby not only was relaxed but also calmly laid an egg on the air. Unflappable!

Ruby is a hen, a mother hen, and nurturing is what she is all about. When I got her, she was at the bottom of the chicken totem pole, the last to enter the flock. Now, four years later, she is the matron. She spent yesterday being an "aunt." Two of my hens had chicks hatching, and Ruby stayed in the brood house with them the entire day. The results of her midwifing are two black chicks and two red ones. Ruby spent the night sleeping in the horse stall by herself rather than in the coop with the others. She needed some well-deserved rest.

I have no idea why Ruby is the way she is, except that I know she's on a mission. She has changed people's minds about birds, opened them up to the possibilities of what animals can bring to us. And she has taught me an amazing number of things. When we walk together, she'll share nature with me. If I pick up a rock, she'll show me all the life that's under it. She notices things that, had I not been with her, I would never have seen. She's shown me eagles. She's shown me courage. But most of all, Ruby has shown me that we must never underestimate who animals are—or why they're here.

—MAUREEN FREDRICKSON, VICE PRESIDENT OF PROGRAMS, DELTA SOCIETY

"Birds are the splash of color across the gray winter landscape, the melody of a hundred voices on a spring morning . . . They are the insight gained into the private lives of wild things over years of observation."

MARCUS SCHNECK, AUTHOR OF *THE BIRD FEEDER GUIDE*

KINDRED SPIRITS OFTEN FIND EACH OTHER WHEN THEY ARE NEEDED MOST.

Sometimes It Just Works That Way

Last summer a small cat began visiting the new home we'd just purchased. My hubby tried to scare her away, but every night I'd go outside and sneak food to her. It was quite clear that she was homeless. It was also quite clear that she was pregnant. And then she just disappeared.

I worried about her, but there wasn't much I could do. She wasn't my cat. Then, about a month later, she reappeared. I couldn't take her to the SPCA (Society for the Prevention of Cruelty to Animals)—or even try to find a home for her—because I wasn't sure where her babies were. At least that was what I told myself in the weeks that followed.

Well, it didn't take long before she was pregnant again. It made me sad to think of her and her babies having to be outside in the cold. I was pregnant myself at the time, so I felt a bond with this poor cat. I think she knew it and felt the same way about me.

As it turned out, I lost my baby. But two days after I came home from the hospital, the cat was there trying to get into our house—trying like crazy. I knew this was her way of finding a safe place to give birth. We already had two cats, so my hubby didn't want anything to do with her plight. But because of what I had just gone through, and seeing how upset I was, he agreed to let her have the babies in the house on the condition that after the birth, she would go right to the SPCA with all her kittens.

Well, we are now the proud parents of eight cats. I couldn't bear to part with any; we kept them all. We named the mama cat Willow. Her babies are Pudgie, Bear, Tigger, Piglet, and Matilda—and they all get along with our other two, Moose and Thomas.

The funny thing is, with all that had happened, I thought Willow needed me. But the truth is, I now realize, that I needed Willow more. She pulled me through a really bad time. Giving her and her babies a loving, safe home is the least I can do for what she gave me.

"FOR WILLOW, THE STRONGEST LADY I KNOW."

—LISA VALANCIUS

❧

"Time spent with cats is never wasted."

COLETTE, FRENCH AUTHOR

ANIMALS UNDERSTAND THINGS THAT
HUMANS CAN'T PUT INTO WORDS, WHICH
MAY BE WHY A FERRET NAMED SOSHA KNEW
WHEN HE WAS NEEDED.

Sosha: Therapy Ferret

I have a very special pet ferret named Sosha. I know all people think their pets are special, but Sosha has done something pretty remarkable—especially for a ferret.

A few months ago, a friend of mine brought her mentally disabled four-year-old son, Marc, over to my house for a visit. Now Sosha is very wary of strangers. Also, he doesn't usually stay awake more than an hour or two at a time. But when Marc sat down on the floor, Sosha immediately walked over to the boy and allowed the child to hold and inspect him. He didn't try to play with Marc or to run away as he usually does. Instead, he remained uncharacteristically passive. It was so strange because I'd never seen my ferret allow himself to be held that long. By anyone. He doesn't even let *me* hold him for more than two minutes to be petted.

Sosha seemed to sense that there was something different about this child. He just continued to let Marc pet and hold him. Then, all of a sudden, the boy looked up and blurted out "cat!" It was the first time any of us had heard him speak a single word! My four-year-old daughter tried explaining to Marc that Sosha was a ferret and not a cat. But he didn't care—and neither did his mother or I. We were so excited that he had said something. Sosha had reached him somehow, and made a connection. Marc now comes over every week for "ferret therapy."

I don't know if it's that Sosha is a special ferret or just that Marc believes he is, but there is a bond between the two that is inexplicable. I've heard stories before about dogs making a connection with people who are afflicted with different disorders, but I never dreamed a ferret could do the same. In fact, Sosha now seems to know when Marc is coming over and stays awake and with him whenever he's here.

Since that first breakthrough moment, Marc has come remarkably far with his speech. He now makes a genuine effort to talk to the ferret. He still calls him a cat, but I don't think Sosha minds one bit! And as far as I'm concerned, a healing animal by any name is still a miracle worker.

—KATHY SMITH

❧

"People listen with their ears, but an animal hears with its heart."

HEART SONG

58

A LOVING ANIMAL CAN MAKE A LIFETIME OF DIFFERENCE IN A LONELY WORLD— ESPECIALLY WHEN IT KEEPS A PROMISE.

The Loving Cat Who Kept His Word

I live in an "old folks" home with my best friend and roommate, Elijah. Now, Elijah is a gray-striped tabby cat. He is only 3 years old. I am 63 and, I thought, a member of a superior species. However, we compete daily to see who is really running the place.

My former neighbor, Helen, just loved Elijah. She came by at least twice a day to visit him. Being the affectionate gentleman cat he is, Elijah reveled in her attention.

Helen was always ready to cat-sit whenever I was away for a few days.

The other residents thought Helen was different. True, she was slightly mentally challenged, had never married, had very few friends and no apparent relatives, and was always ready to argue. But she loved animals, especially my pal, Elijah.

You could say, Helen and I were somehow bonded by our mutual love for my cat.

When Helen became extremely ill, she was sent across the street to a board-and-care facility to die.

Three weeks later, I discovered she had no visitors in the weeks she had been there. I promptly put Elijah in his cat carrier and took him over to visit her.

I very gently set him on the foot of her bed and opened the carrier door. Being in a strange, new place, he cautiously peeked outside. As soon as Elijah heard Helen's voice, he ran across the bed to her. And her welcome was as heartfelt as always.

Elijah and I visited Helen about three or four times a week. The head nurse asked if I would take him to visit other animal-loving patients. I became a volunteer and loved seeing the dismal faces brighten into smiles whenever I knocked on a door and said, "Elijah is here to see you!"

I know my cat enjoyed all the extra attention. I always had a hard time getting him back into his cat carrier.

Of course, we did spend most of our time with Helen. She would always end the visits by holding Elijah close to her and say to him, "Elijah, my dear friend, I don't want to die alone. . . . Will you please be with me when I go?" He would always answer her with a wagging tail and a long, loving purr.

I got the call at 11:30 on a warm night. Helen was calling for Elijah. We hurried over there. Our friend did not look good, but a sweet smile came over her tired face when she saw Elijah. She held out her arms for him.

They did their usual loving routine for the last time. Then Helen's tired arms slowly slipped away from around Elijah. Her eyes closed, and she just went away. Elijah smelled her forehead, cheeks, nose, and lips for a few moments. He gave a sad little meow as if to say, "Goodbye my friend." He looked at me for a moment, and then with no persuasion from me, Elijah slowly walked back to his cat carrier.

Elijah's friend Helen did not die alone.

—LeGrand Day, columnist, *Los Angeles Daily News*

❥

"There are two means of refuge from the miseries of life: music and cats."

Albert Schweitzer, French philosopher and physician

WHOEVER SAID ANIMALS DON'T BELONG IN
A CLASSROOM HAS A LOT TO LEARN.

Classroom Ferret

I introduced Syoud to my classroom of second and third graders last year. Before buying her, we studied different pets and considered the time and materials each would need to be kept healthy and happy—necessary research for anyone planning to adopt a member of another species. Once we decided on a ferret, we studied books on how to make her welcome and safe in our classroom, and she has since become a wonderful addition to the school. Her name means "thief" in our local Native American language. Ferrets love to steal and hide small objects (particularly under furniture and other unreachable places). Syoud's thievery, though, is of a different nature; she has stolen hearts.

Syoud comes to class with me every day. As gentle and playful with the students as they are with her, she visits the kindergarten classrooms, goes out to recess on her leash, and has been known to keep 327 children from getting to their buses on time.

One day last year, Syoud helped turn a life around. My class had gone to music study in another part of the school. I was alone going over test papers when an older boy with many behavior problems suddenly ducked into the room. He had not seen me sitting there and was obviously trying to hide.

I knew this boy, his family, and the hell he lived in. He was extremely capable of violence; he had been very well taught. Suspecting that he was running from something, I greeted him calmly and asked why he had dropped in.

"Oh, just wanted to say hi," he said, looking quickly out the window and ducking down onto a chair that would put him below window height.

"Well, while you are here, would you like to hold Syoud?" I asked.

He looked uneasy. "Will she bite?"

"Not if you are kind to her," I said. I lifted Syoud from her cage. She was very sleepy and cuddly as I handed her to him.

The boy took Syoud and cradled her in his lap. I sat down beside them.

We didn't talk. The boy just stroked Syoud as she slowly woke up. Drowsily, she nuzzled his neck and stuck her soft nose in his ear. He smiled at her sniffing and snooping. Before long his stiff posture relaxed. I could see it in his jaw, his shoulders, the ease and gentleness in which his hands glided along Syoud's coat. Something remarkable was taking place. Whether it was trust or friendship or simple unspoken understanding, it was something that he clearly had never experienced before. After a while, as if her work were done, Syoud climbed from his shoulder up my hand to my neck.

I quietly asked the boy if he needed to be somewhere. He nodded, saying that maybe he should see Carl, the school counselor. He accepted my offer to accompany him with Syoud on our way to pick up my class from music. Later I learned what had happened. The boy had run from his class after pitching another student across the teacher's desk into a window, vowing to go home and get a gun. I do not doubt there was a gun in this boy's home or that he was capable of using it. He was on his way there when he ducked into my room. I also do not doubt that if it hadn't been for his en-counter with Syoud, and the silent connection they made, he would have carried out his threat.

People wonder why I want pets in a classroom. I wonder why people don't!

—SANDRA HUNT, AN ELEMENTARY SCHOOL TEACHER
IN A NATIVE AMERICAN SCHOOL

❥

"I sing for them, the animals."

ANONYMOUS, *I SING FOR THE ANIMALS* (TETON SIOUX)

THERE ARE ANIMALS THAT ARE BORN TO
HEAL; WE PEOPLE CAN TAKE NONE OF THE
CREDIT. NOR SHOULD WE.

Falstaff and Troi: A Couple of Healing Tails

One of my partners in animal-assisted therapy (AAT) is Falstaff, a Great Dane–boxer mix. On this particular day, we were in a psychiatric unit, making the rounds, when a nurse asked us to visit one woman in particular. Jean had been hospitalized for several days without any change and had totally withdrawn into herself. Her eyes were glazed, she did not speak, she did not even move on her own; in fact, she needed to be guided in all her actions.

I stood by while the nurse placed Falstaff in front of Jean. The nurse then took one of Jean's hands and helped her stroke Falstaff's head, all the while talking to her about the dog. After two or three minutes, Jean raised her head and looked at the nurse. It was the first direct eye contact she had made! Her expression appeared somewhat startled, but she said clearly, "Where am I?"

"In a hospital," the nurse answered gently. "Where did you think you were?"

Jean responded, "In hell!"

Apparently Jean's concept of hell did not include animals. Seeing and touching Falstaff had jolted her back into the world and reality. She began to improve from that moment on.

On another occasion, Falstaff entered the psychiatric unit and saw an elderly woman hunched over in a chair. He focused on her immediately, going directly to her side. Then he just sat there, gazing steadily at her. I knelt beside him. He obviously had a mission and was taking care of what he knew he needed to do. Sarah, though slumped over, saw the dog and reached toward him.

Gently, she cupped Falstaff's head in both her hands. She then slowly bent forward and rested her forehead on Falstaff's forehead. For nearly 15 minutes, Sarah and Falstaff remained in that position

Sarah sobbed from her soul, but she didn't let go of Falstaff. Neither did Falstaff twitch a muscle—he remained where he was, where he knew he was most needed. Soon the staff was crying, moved by what they were witnessing; it was a time beyond human intervention.

Finally, Sarah sat back and Falstaff slowly moved away. I have no idea what passed between them. I don't have to know. But I do remember that the expression on her face after their time together seemed to be wonderfully peaceful. I cannot always explain what my animal companions do for me when we're together. I just know that my soul feels better when I open myself to them. I have absolutely no doubt that Falstaff gave Sarah his own kind of healing

Troi, a Portuguese water dog, had her own kind of healing, too. She was a new member of my family, and I was excited about the prospect of our making visits to the hospital together. As her skills developed, I alerted the occupational therapist on the Rehabilitation Unit that Troi would soon be ready to participate in animal-assisted therapy. I even bragged a little—Troi was my first dog who was a retriever, and I knew that fetch games could be very useful in rehabilitation.

On our first visit, the occupational therapist had carefully chosen Helen for us to work with. Helen was recovering from a stroke and had limited use of her right side. Being right-handed, she was highly sensitive about her new disability. She did *not* want to participate in therapy, and—dog or no dog—that day was no exception. The therapist cajoled her into at least trying.

Helen protested but finally agreed to try to throw a toy for Troi to retrieve. Helen had to work very hard, and she managed to throw the toy only about two feet in front of her. Embarrassed, she began to insist that she be taken back to her room. Then she noticed that Troi had *not* gone for the toy. Well, did I have egg on my face! Here I had talked about what a great retriever Troi was, and now the dog was just sitting there.

We all decided we needed to do something to get Troi to retrieve the toy—though we didn't know what the something was. We devised a variety of strategies to encourage Troi to pick up the toy. Nothing worked. Every time Helen threw the toy, it was I who retrieved it—not Troi.

Then suddenly we all realized something: Helen was throwing the toy! As soon as our focus had shifted from her to Troi, Helen relaxed and began to get involved in the therapy session. Troi just sat by Helen's side, refusing to move except to blink at us. After about five minutes, Troi apparently decided that she had given us enough time to think that we had trained her—and she began to fetch. By now, Helen was relaxed and having fun—and reveling in the fact that she had gotten Troi to fetch.

I believe that on some level Troi knew what Helen needed, so she took the pressure off Helen and placed the attention on herself. Because of Troi, Helen gained the infusion of confidence necessary to put her on the road to recovery. We people can take none of the credit.

—ANN R. HOWIE, A.C.S.W.,
AAT SERVICES MANAGER,
DELTA SOCIETY

❧

*"A doctor may heal the body,
but an animal can heal the soul."*

HEART SONG

SOME LOVE POEMS ARE MORE
DEEPLY FELT THAN OTHERS.
I BELIEVE THIS IS ONE OF THEM.

The Leader Dog

*I often sit and wonder why I can't see like you
I often wonder what you're like, they say your eyes are
    blue.*

*But I don't know just what that means, my picture is not
    clear
I only know I feel your glow and love to know you're near.*

*When I go to bed at night, no need to light the room
for just to know you're here with me can chase the darkest
    gloom.*

*I say my little prayer at night, for kids across the blue
though they can see, I'm better off because I still have you.*

69

You know I love you very much, you've given me your
  sight
instead of running round all day, I hold your reins so
  tight.

I pray to God to keep you safe the way that you keep me
Oh how I wish I had my sight, so that you could run free.

—M. A. ROUND (1966)

❧

"There is an inherent poetry to having a guide dog."
STEVE KUUSISTO, AUTHOR OF *PLANET OF THE BLIND*

WHEN YOUR PETS KNOW MORE THAN YOU
DO ABOUT MATTERS OF THE HEART, IT'S
TIME TO PAY ATTENTION.

For the Sake of the Cat

I'm fond of saying that each of my four cats has a job. The job is a self-appointed task in each case, like anything else a cat does, and is taken very seriously.

My youngest cat, Worthless, is an add-on to our alarm clock. As soon as she hears it ring, she leaps into our bed (if she's not already there) and begins squalling. Next comes dancing on sensitive portions of human anatomy. If this fails to get lazy humans up and about, she bumps her nose into mine or nips gently. We haven't been able to sneak an extra five minutes rest since this cat was five months old. She's dedicated.

Eclipse, Worthless's mom, looks like she could be a wizard's familiar but has the more down-to-earth job of rodent control engineer. She'd been living as a stray when we took her in, and being well-fed hasn't dulled her hunting instincts. Every time I hear that sharp little "Eee-eee-eeee," I know she's caught another mouse before it got into my kitchen.

Gandalf, my male Persian, no relation to any of the others, keeps the furniture from walking out of the room on its own. I'm not sure what job title you'd assign him, but, cat-like, he's very serious about it. He firmly believes that just as long as he sleeps on each sofa, chair, or table for part of the day, it will never be able to leave. He dedicates his entire life to this proposition with so much success that you almost never see him awake.

Velvet, our senior cat, is our marriage counselor. Whenever we raise our voices to each other (married couples, or at least my husband and I, argue from across a room), Velvet dances frenetically, then walks between us and strikes each set of ankles in turn. Then she makes a whole series of squalls, squawks, and rumbles that mean "I'm upset and want you to stop!" If we don't, she yells at us. Yes, yells. Moreover, she speaks two words of English, which, although she speaks them with a pronounced feline accent, isn't bad for a cat. She yells "no" (pronouncing it "ni-ow") and "uh-uh" (pronouncing it "waiow-uh"). I'd think I was imagining it if it hadn't happened so many times during our 13-year marriage, which started when Velvet was 4.

It isn't that we fight a lot. Every marriage is subject to spats: the pick-your-stuff-up argument, the why'd-you-do-that argument, the why-didn't-you-do-that argument. You can talk yourself into the idea that these squabbles are a serious sign of incompatibility if you don't take the chance to cool off, to consider your next words, to think about what you're about to say and why.

That's what Velvet does for us, by fearless intervention. She's our referee, making sure that we don't get outside the rules of civilized marital discourse. She knows, with feline dedication, that her people belong together and talking softly—not across from each other and shouting. At the merest sound of a raised voice, she dashes in. Pretty soon, we're apologizing and hugging, long before any serious harm is done. Can't upset the cat.

Velvet is 17 years old now and as important to us as if she were our child; certainly, she's ours by her own choice. But she won't need to work at her job forever; we've learned a few things about not letting a little spat turn into a tidal wave. They're simple rules: Speak softly to one another, ask instead of accusing, treat each other with the courtesy and kindness you would show a stranger. Anything else hurts children and other living things—including both of you.

Blessed are the peacemakers, for they are . . . sometimes cats.

"FOR VELVET"
—MARGARET R. CARTWRIGHT

❧

"An animal's eyes have the power
to speak a great language."
MARTIN BUBER, AUSTRIAN PHILOSOPHER

AN OLD DOG SHOWED HER A NEW
WAY OF LIFE—AND GAVE HER THE COURAGE
TO GO ON LIVING IT TO THE FULLEST
WITH ANOTHER.

Tennis Anyone?

I found out about service dogs very much by accident. Literally. I'd had multiple sclerosis (MS) for almost 20 years, but it had just gotten to where my limitations were really affecting my lifestyle. I wasn't going out by myself. I was relying on my family to do things for me, like really simple things. I needed help getting dressed, help walking, actually, help with just about everything. My children felt they were like my caretakers, and so did my husband, and that wasn't the relationship I wanted with them.

Then one day I fell down. The pet dog we had at the time, Casper, a 10-year-old Samoyed-Lab mix that we'd gotten from a shelter just a few months before, came and laid down next to me. Without any encouragement or command, he helped me get up. At the time I didn't know what he was doing and kept trying to push him away, only I didn't have the strength in my arms. What he did was roll me over, and I hung on to him; then he got up and that pulled me up. I thought, "Hey, *this* is what I need!"

Casper became my first service dog. We had adopted him because my daughter, who was three at the time, had developed a fear of dogs. To get her to overcome it, we had gone through months of me driving her to the shelter, stopping in the parking lot and then driving away, each time getting closer and closer to where the dogs actually were. And then we met Casper. He was just an exquisite animal—like a human in a dog suit, except with a lot more perception than most people.

Casper worked with me for three months and then he died. It was totally unexpected. He had cancer that we hadn't known about. We got the diagnosis one day, and he died the next. It was devastating. I'd gotten very, very attached to him. It wasn't just our working together; he was simply a wonderful creature.

A few days later, I went back to the shelter to tell them what had happened and to get a picture they had of Casper, because I had no other photograph of him. It was difficult being there. I really didn't think I had room in my heart for another dog. Losing Casper had been extremely painful. But, at the same time, I also knew that I had these limitations, and now I was right back where I was before I had begun working with him. People were going to be helping me again, and the thought was not pleasant.

One of the shelter workers who knew me encouraged me to go out to see the dogs; talked me into it, really. I went reluctantly. I wasn't looking for a dog. I was just sort of being nice.

It was awful. All the dogs started barking, "Take me home. Take me home." I was just about to leave when I noticed this huge dog—a German shepherd–Great Dane mix—in this little kennel. (Any kennel would have been little with him in it.) I remarked casually, "Looks like a nice dog." And the woman said, "Well, actually that's the dog I thought might be appropriate for you. His name is Joe." I was like, Well, I'm here. I suppose I can take him out.

Joe apparently had no formal—or for that matter informal—training, because he was totally oblivious to even meek requests from me. He did allow me to walk him without pulling, which seemed to surprise the people at the shelter who said he was ordinarily a rough-and-tumble guy. But he was walking along very nicely with me, almost politely. I think I had "sucker" written across my forehead.

"He doesn't seem to know how to do anything," I said.

"Oh, you can work with him," they said.

I stayed with him for quite a long time. Then I brought my family back the next day to see if he was amenable to the children, and my husband, and if there were any blatant things that would rule him out as a member of our household. Nothing showed up. "Okay," I said. "We'll give it a shot."

We stuffed Joe in our van (he couldn't even turn around

in it—he was *that* big) and took him home. I started working with him immediately.

I am not a professional dog trainer. I never even had a lot of experience with recreational obedience. I once trained a beagle that I had to the point where he could work off lead and was very reliable. (I was so naive. Nobody had ever told me that a beagle was like a nose on a string.) But a service dog is different.

Casper hadn't needed anything. He was perfect. He'd carry and retrieve things for me. He'd help me to balance and to walk, which was major because I'd fall so often. Alleviating that fear of falling and preventing me from getting hurt was his main job—and he did it brilliantly.

Now, here was Joe. I thought, well he's tall enough—29 inches at the shoulder—so he's going to help me to walk. Then I started thinking about all sorts of other things he could help me with. "Yeah," I told myself, "I could teach a dog to do that." I look back now and I think, "What was I thinking?"

First, I had to teach Joe basic obedience—to sit, lie down, and stay. I felt that if I could have that kind of control, no matter how crazy things got we'd have something to fall back on for a time out together. I'd told the shelter that I would keep him for six weeks, but if he didn't work out, I was going to have to bring him back and get another dog. They understood my situation. Unfortunately, Joe didn't.

At 5½ weeks I started saying to him, "Pack your bones. Get ready 'cause you're going back. We have 72 hours here, buddy, and you're going back." And it was like all of a sudden—boom—he got it!

He was good about retrieving and picking up most things because I drop things a lot. The way the MS affects me is that I have poor balance and frequent visual deficits—sometimes I'm totally blind. I'm also numb, so it's hard to get a good grip on anything, and my muscles are weak. It's a combination that makes you look as if you're a little tipsy most of the time.

I was trying to teach Joe to pick up everything because there are times when I need that. He was great at picking up some things, but he absolutely—flatly—refused to pick up my cane. I thought, "What's the deal? This is a stick!" And his answer was, "Yeah, well it's your stick. You want it? You get it."

That's what *he* thought. I had a plan.

Joe was obsessed with tennis balls; no problem getting him to retrieve them. So I took a tennis ball, cut Xs in both ends, and put it on the shaft of my cane. And it worked! Joe would pick up the tennis ball, picking up my cane by default. But for months I walked around with a cane that had this grubby, disgusting tennis ball on it. I'm real short, only five feet tall, so here's this chick, and she's kind of weaving down the sidewalk, and she's got this huge dog and this stick with a tennis ball stuck on it. People would look at me and not know what to ask about first, because they somehow feel compelled to make conversation—and I could see them thinking, "What's it safe to talk about?" So they would focus on the tennis ball. They'd say, "That's an interesting thing." And I'd say, "It was a terrible tennis accident." That would usually end the conversation.

Eventually, I couldn't stand the tennis ball on my cane anymore, so I got smaller and smaller balls until Joe's mouth went on either side of it and he was actually grabbing the cane. Then we just lost the ball.

I've had Joe seven years. In 1993 he won the Delta Society's Service Animal of the Year award. (That's how I found out about Delta Society. I loved them so much I volunteered to work with them and have been working with them ever since.) At the time, there was a huge amount of controversy about whether people could—or should—train their own service dogs. There still is controversy about this—whether it is legal, whether it is safe. My answer is an unequivocal yes. And Joe is my unequivocal proof!

—SUSAN DUNCAN

❧

*"A dog is the only thing on this earth
that loves you more than he loves himself."*

JOSH BILLINGS (HENRY WHEELER SHAW),
AMERICAN HUMORIST

Voices

"I'm a survivor of a serious heart defect
and a recovered battered wife. Animals
routinely save my life."

NAME WITHHELD

❧

"Animals don't avert their eyes because they can't
bear to see your pain. My 13-year-old dog has
always been here to offer me comfort and love.
Unconditionally."

JULIE RAND

❧

"I don't think there's an antidepressant drug that
works faster to lift your spirits than a purring cat
in your lap."

JILL KAVNER

❧

"We travel around the world. When I play in a concert, he sits on the floor, next to or under my chair. We go everywhere, and at home, at night, he is right there on my bed. He is my eyes; he is my soul mate."

STACY BLAIR, a blind classical trumpet player, talking about Guthrie, his golden retriever guide dog

Parenting Paradoxes and Pet Pals

*"My father was a Saint Bernard, my mother was a collie,
but I am a Presbyterian."*

MARK TWAIN, AMERICAN WRITER

HE WAS A DOG-EARED CAT WITH A SECRET
IDENTITY THAT CAME TO LIFE BY
ACCIDENT.

A Tale of Two Kitties

They say that cats have nine lives. Well, I don't know about that. But I do know one cat who had two lives. His name was Smokey; at least that's what I called him. He was a gray-striped tom with a pink nose, four white paws, and a silky-furred right ear that folded over at the tip. I found him shivering in our garage as a kitten when I was nine years old and kept him hidden in my bedroom for a week until I was sure my mom would let me keep him. A stranger might not have thought he was much to look at, but to me he was the cutest kitten in the world. My mother used to joke about how I was the only girl in Indian Hills, Colorado, who'd fall in love with a "dog-eared" cat.

By the time I was 11, Smokey had pretty much established his own daily routine of running out and about in the daytime, always returning home in time for dinner, after which he'd curl up on my bed. When I'd slip beneath the covers for the night, he'd move close to my face, nudge his head right under my chin, and purr like a warm, small-appliance motor. I never had a bad dream when Smokey slept beside me. He liked my three brothers, but it was obvious that he was a one-kid cat. And I was his girl. Or so I thought.

One night that July, Smokey didn't come home. I was upset, but my mother assured me it wasn't unusual for a cat to wander off for an adventure now and then. I spent the next few days searching for him, calling his name and expecting any minute to see him, but there was no sign of him. By the end of the week, we were all upset.

My mother agreed that I should go to the general store and put up a "Missing" notice with Smokey's picture. I picked out one where he was lying sphinxlike across my pillow; his bent ear and white paws clearly visible. When I wrote down his coloring and distinguishing marks, it was hard to keep from crying.

My brother Dave went with me to the store to post the notice for Smokey. Once it was up, we stood back to see if it was in a good spot. Well, it was in a good spot, all right. It was right next to a notice for another missing cat, "Ranger"—and the only difference between them was their names. Their descriptions were identical.

I wrote down the phone number and called the moment we got home. The girl who answered said that her missing cat, Ranger, always stayed out at night and came home in the morning but hadn't shown up in a week. I told her that my cat, Smokey—same coloring, same bent right ear—went out in the morning and came home in the evening and that he hadn't shown up in a week. It was a little too much of a co-incidence to be a coincidence. With an unspoken twinge of betrayal, we both conceded that her Ranger and my Smokey were one and the same cat—and that he had been living a double life! So much for a one-kid cat. But two-timing tom or not, both of us loved him, and he was still missing.

The girl's name was Evelyn Boldoven, and we arranged to meet the following day. She was a year older than I, which was probably why we hadn't known each other even though she lived just a quarter of a mile away. She brought over her pictures of Ranger, and I brought out my pictures of Smokey. We spent the afternoon sharing stories about "our dog-eared, one-kid cat," alternately sniffling and laughing at the similarity of his two-household antics. By dinnertime we'd gone through more than half a box of Kleenex and had become best friends.

Evelyn and I handmade flyers for our missing cat ("an-swers to the name of Smokey or Ranger"), passed them out all around town, and kept each other from giving up hope by recounting amazing stories of lost animals who'd miracu-lously found their way home after years. But by the end of August, even these took on a hollow ring.

Then, a week before school started, we got a phone call that seemed too good to be true. It was from a woman in Golden, a town about 10 miles away, saying she'd seen our flyer in a gas station and believed she had our cat. Her son had found it about a month ago on the side of the road, bloody and near death from an animal attack, and she'd been nursing it back to health. She said that she'd named him "Marker" because of his bent ear.

My mother drove Evelyn and me to Golden that same afternoon, cautioning us not to get too excited in case the cat wasn't ours. How many dog-eared cats could there be? We wondered but really didn't want to know. Holding hands and squeezing tightly, we followed the woman into the house where she said Marker was resting. But the moment we saw him there was no doubt that Marker wasn't Marker. He was Smokey. He was Ranger. He was ours, and he was alive! His nonstop purring all the way home told us that he was as happy to be found as we were to find him.

Smokey/Ranger continued to live his two lives—dividing his days and nights and love between Evelyn's house and ours—until advancing age and illness curtailed him. When his health worsened, we knew the kindest thing to do was to set him free from his suffering. Evelyn and I were with him when he died. He seemed to know we were both there— stroking his white paws, caressing his bent ear—and he drifted from us peacefully, purring to the end.

No, Smokey wasn't the one-kid cat I once thought he was. He was just the best cat that ever was.

—JUNE TORENCE

P.S. Evelyn, who's remained my best friend for all these years, says the same thing about Ranger.

INTERSPECIES PARENTING CAN BE
CONFUSING FOR ALL INVOLVED,
ESPECIALLY WHEN A HUMAN
HAS TO TEACH A BIRD TO FLY.

A Pigeon Named Howard

My daughter found the young pigeon on a downtown sidewalk in Baltimore. He had flown into a plate-glass window and couldn't get up. Knowing that my husband and I had rehabilitated two injured pigeons in recent years, she wrapped this one gently in her scarf and brought him home.

The little guy was frightened. Even though he looked fully grown, I could tell that he wasn't; he was still making his baby peeping noises. My husband felt the bird's legs and knew right away that one of the upper thighbones was broken. We quickly made a sling for him out of old rags and suspended his body from the top of a small holding cage, stationing him carefully by putting towels around bricks so he could not move. Needless to say, Howard, as we named him, was not too happy about his enforced holding pattern, but he had to put up with this inconvenience in order to heal.

After four or five days, we took Howard out of the sling, and he immediately fell on his beak. But he got right up and, even though he was very wobbly, was able to stand on his own two feet. Before long, he was happily hobbling around. Three weeks later, he seemed strong enough to be set free.

We took Howard up to our local shopping center where all the other pigeons hang out and tried to let him go. We threw him up in the air, but he just fluttered a bit and landed back on my husband's shoulder. It was obvious that Howard needed flying lessons.

We brought him back home and set up a ladder in the basement. It was there that we gave him his flying lessons. I would stand a few yards away, and Howard would fly to the ladder. After a couple of weeks of flying lessons, Howard's wings had increased significantly in strength. He could fly back and forth, high and low, with ease. He was ready to leave our nest. Or so we thought.

The next time we tried to let him go, my husband spotted a hawk lurking close by. Afraid that Howard might be the hawk's next meal, we brought him back home. Another week went by. Again we tried. We threw him up in the air, and he flew around in two small circles before landing back on my husband's shoulder once again. Flight was obviously not in Howard's plan. He ended up becoming a permanent member of our family.

I suppose Howard thought we were his parents, which in a way we were—and are. He turned out to be a wonderful pet. He will always have a limp, but that does not hinder him in any way. He loves us to pet him and always "hoots" when he hears our voices. Our friends are amazed that he immediately flies to us when we call him. He lives in our bird room, which he shares with 10 others. During the day, he's loose (free as a bird), but we put him in his own cage at night.

A few months ago, though, we got a big surprise from our little home-loving pigeon. It seems that Howard is really a "Howie." She laid two eggs and has laid many more since. Howie celebrated her first birthday with us this month. We're looking forward to many more. I know there are a lot of people who think of pigeons as dirty pests, but they would sure change their minds if they got to meet a wonderful pet like our adorable Howie.

—PATRICIA SINGLE

❧

"Man is the two-legged animal without feathers."

PLATO, GREEK PHILOSOPHER

HE WAS AN L.A. POOCH WHO PROVED
THAT THE TRUTH ABOUT CATS
AND DOGS IS A LIE.

Scruffy and Josephine

I was taking our dog, Scruffy, for a walk one day when suddenly, from out of nowhere, this small, pearl gray, long-haired cat appeared on the sidewalk. Scruffy looked at the cat, the cat looked at Scruffy, and the next thing I knew, the cat had joined us on our walk. She didn't just follow us, she trotted right alongside as if she'd been doing it for years.

For the next three or four days, every time I would take Scruffy out, this little gray girl cat would be waiting. And Scruffy loved her. He'd see her, and his tail would start swirling like a propeller. She would put her head right up to his nose, and he'd sort of nuzzle her; it was their special greeting.

One day while we were on our walk, two mangy-looking dogs started coming down the street toward us. Suddenly Scruffy, who was probably the most laid-back, sweet-tempered dog in all of Los Angeles, put himself in front of the cat and began barking ferociously until those other dogs ran away.

After that, the cat not only walked with us but also followed us home every day. I knew we couldn't keep her, at least not in the house, because my wife, Marsha, is allergic to cats. Of course, we had already made the inevitable mistake of feeding her. We might not have wanted to make a commitment, but it was pretty obvious that the cat had adopted us. Then we began calling her Josephine—the next thing I knew, I was building a house for her out in our garage.

Scruffy and Josephine walked together every day for nearly four years and never tired of each other's company. Their cat-dog friendship was a life lesson in getting along. When we had to move to New York, we were heartsick that we couldn't take Josephine with us. Our one consolation was that we did find a great home for her with a neighbor whose female cat had recently died leaving a male companion lonely and eager for company.

Scruffy and Josephine both passed away two years ago. We like to think that they're now happily walking together, forever.

—LARRY FERBER

❧

"When dogs are happy, they don't have to bother smiling. They just wag their tails."

BIL KEANE, AMERICAN CARTOONIST

The Oddest Couple in Town

Having a dog in Indian Hills during the last years of the 1950s was like having an outhouse; everyone had one. The bigger the dog, the bigger the bragging rights. Fortunately, our family wasn't into bragging. We had Peewee, a fat little Chihuahua who was a threat to no one but himself.

The one thing Peewee had going for him was speed; he was the fastest dog in the neighborhood. There wasn't any that he couldn't outrun. His short, stubby legs were virtually turbocharged, and they saved his life many times.

Peewee had, to put it mildly, an inflated sense of self. Despite his diminutive size, he had the confidence of a Rottweiler and the ego of a Doberman. When he looked in the mirror, he saw a mastiff. He was afraid of nothing and thought it his mission in life to take on all comers. This, unfortunately, led to many fights and numerous trips to the vet. The fights always ended the same way, with Peewee, tail between his legs, racing home—luckily outdistancing his adversaries before they could do him serious harm.

This was Peewee's way of life-on-the-edge until Black Jack, a beautiful one-eyed German shepherd came along. Black Jack belonged to an itinerant family of 12 that lived down the road. The father was a brutish ex-Marine whose ill temper and right foot was the cause of Black Jack's monovision. But despite the abuse that this dog endured, he was as gentle and even-tempered an animal as any I've ever known—except when it came to looking after Peewee, which became his life's work from the moment they met.

Peewee and Black Jack were instant and almost inseparable friends, and an odd couple they made. Every morning Black Jack would walk up the road to our house, scratch on the door until Mom let Peewee out, and off they would go. Peewee would pick a fight with every dog they met. The moment the barks turned to bites, he would run for home, and Black Jack would finish the fight, miraculously coming away with barely a scratch.

That's how it was—Peewee out looking for trouble and Black Jack looking out for Peewee—until one morning when Black Jack didn't show up. We weren't worried that first day, and I don't remember if even Peewee noticed his pal's absence. But two days later, I decided to go down the hill to find out where Black Jack was.

When I got there, I knew that something was wrong. The door to the house was slightly ajar, and when I looked inside, it was empty. With back rent due and unpaid bills, the family had packed their belongings and skipped town. I ran home crying that we would never see Black Jack again. In the days that followed, Peewee knew something was wrong, too. Instead of bounding off as usual, he'd just walk outside in the morning and look around, then come back and lie down by the door.

About a week later, on my way home from school, I was walking past the abandoned house where Black Jack had lived and saw Peewee barking at the cellar door. At first I thought he was just missing his friend. But when I got closer, I heard something else—it was a scratching sound. I tried to open the door, but it was locked. I bent down and peered into the small cellar window. There wasn't much light, but there was enough for me to see what I hardly dared to believe I was seeing. It was Black Jack, dirty and weak, leaning against the door. I pulled out the window, climbed through and dropped to the floor. Within seconds my arms were around him, and I was crying. He was wet and smelled foul, but I was never happier to see anyone in my life. And I'm pretty sure the feeling was mutual.

At first Dad said we couldn't keep Black Jack, but he finally gave in and told us that we could as long as he would be an "outside dog"; he wasn't to be allowed in the house. Well, Black Jack had a way of getting to people as well as to dogs. It didn't take long before Dad forgot his edict. A week later, Peewee and Black Jack were not only spending their days running in tandem around the neighborhood, they were spending their nights curled up together in the living room as well. And they continued to do so for a very long time.

—RON VANWARMER

❧

"To err is human, to forgive canine."

ANONYMOUS

Elephants and Aunts

When Karha, a baby Asiatic elephant, was born in December of 1995, she was quite the pachyderm bundle of joy at the Chester Zoo—weighing in at 230 pounds (104 kilos)! It had been 20 years since the birth of Jubilee, the very first Asiatic elephant born in the United Kingdom, and although others were born afterward, none, unfortunately, had survived. With less than 40,000 of these magnificent creatures left in the wild, everyone at Chester was thrilled with the arrival of Karha. Everyone, that is, except her mother, Thi Hi Way.

Though large in size and personality, Thi Hi Way was short on maternal instinct. She rejected Karha at birth, a critical period for newborns of any species, refusing to nurse or nurture her. This meant a daily, round-the-clock watch on Karha with a keeper always on hand. A baby—even a thick-skinned, 230-pound one—needed special care, and that's what Karha received. During the critical early weeks, a specially made coat kept her warm as did the keepers who took turns sleeping beside her.

After a month, Karha was ready to meet the other elephants. Our three senior females, Sheba, Jangoli, and Kumara, became her adoptive "aunts." They are known to the staff as the Mothers' Union because of their instinctual maternal behavior, which they immediately demonstrated with Karha.

Although she wasn't her mother's darling, Karha quickly became the public's favorite and a major attraction at the zoo. A generous donation provided her with a special elephant "nursery" with a built-in bath, and she began to thrive. By her first birthday, she had more than doubled her birth weight and was drinking as much as 16 liters of milk each day. Her image adorned T-shirts, magnets, glasses, and dozens of theme gifts at the zoo shops. She relished the attention. And Thi Hi Way, guided by Sheba and the Mothers' Union, was learning to accept her daughter. It appeared as if things couldn't be going better.

Then one day Karha did what juveniles, regrettably, often do. She put something in her mouth that she shouldn't have—and accidentally swallowed it. Her appetite diminished and she became very ill. The x-rays showed that she had swallowed a stone from the paddock; an operation was risky but necessary.

For days after the surgery, keepers once again slept with Karha around the clock. They didn't mind. They didn't even mind when she awoke from the anesthetic and mistook their TV for a toy (which was about all it was good for after she got through with it). After a few weeks, she was back basking in her public's attention. But she wasn't eating well and certainly not enough. The keepers weighed her daily, but the numbers on the scale were going down instead of up. The veterinary staff did all they could, but it wasn't enough. Sadly, Karha died before reaching a second birthday.

Everyone mourned—even the dauntless Mothers' Union seemed to sense Karha's absence. The only candle of brightness was that Thi Hi Way was once again pregnant, and there was once again a chance for a successful birth.

As New Year's Eve 1997 dawned in the Elephant House, there was great excitement among the residents and the staff. The long wait of nearly two years was almost over. The usual early morning routine was abandoned. This was not going to be an ordinary day, and all in earshot knew it. Suddenly, loud trumpeting announced that something quite momentous had happened. Thi Hi Way had given birth to another daughter, a sturdy female weighing 220 pounds—and a full-blood sister to Karha!

Chang, the baby's father, and Jubilee, the other male in the group, showed little interest in the new arrival. But the Mothers' Union led by Sheba gave the baby a very enthusiastic welcome.

The keeping staff watched anxiously as Thi bent over her new daughter. Her past performance as a mother had been less than stellar, and they were not sure how she would react to her new calf. In those initial moments, there was a lot of breath holding. And then Thi began to nuzzle her new daughter, drawing her close and then closer with each gentle sway of her trunk. A communal sigh of relief was audible. Clearly, Thi was going to be a loving and protective mother—though she had a lot to learn.

It was heartwarming to see Thi being so affectionate. But affection alone wasn't enough. The baby needed feeding, and neither she nor Thi was quite sure how to go about it. Early feeding is vital, so the keepers immediately gave the new baby a bottle. But teaching this calf to feed from her mother was the goal—and for this they could get no better help or advice than from Auntie Sheba.

As the newborn tried to find her way underneath her mother—Thi had not yet learned that she should stand still—Sheba put her trunk gently around the baby and guided her to the right place. Then she placed her trunk on Thi's shoulder to steady her and supervised the feeding process. Very quickly, mother and baby learned what was needed, and Thi was feeding her daughter almost hourly.

The new baby now needed a name. The three that the keepers liked were Kush-Sakil, which means "supreme beauty"; Sitara, which means "star"; and Sithami, which means "hope." The public, having mourned the loss of Karha, was invited by an evening television program to telephone in their choice of the three names. The winner was Sithami. Hope. It couldn't have been more fitting.

Everyone at Chester was jubilant about the new addition

to the herd—but, again, with exception of one. This time it was a three-year-old elephant named Upali who had arrived from a Zurich zoo about seven months earlier. Since he was the baby of the group, the Mothers' Union had made a great fuss over him. So, after a day or two of watching Sithami getting all the attention, Upali decided action was needed. With all the ingenuity of a typical sibling, he gave the baby a jealous push with his trunk. Unfortunately, for Upali, this did not go unnoticed by Auntie Sheba.

Within moments, Sheba corralled Upali, took him to a corner of the paddock, and gave him a light spanking with her trunk. He was a quick learner of lessons. He nuzzled Sheba to show he was sorry and then walked across to Sithami and simply stood quietly in front of her, as if to say, "See, I can be a good boy."

They are friends now, and both Auntie Sheba and Thi Hi Way make sure they stay that way. And if everything works out . . . well, someday they might become more than "just friends."

—PAT CADE, NORTH OF ENGLAND ZOOLOGICAL SOCIETY

❧

"When you have got an elephant by the hind legs and he is trying to run away, it is best to let him run."

ABRAHAM LINCOLN, AMERICAN PRESIDENT

WHEN AN ANIMAL BONDS HEART AND SOUL
TO ANOTHER, IT'S NOT DIFFICULT TO PASS
ON LESSONS IN LOVE.

A Love Tale

We weren't looking for a squirrel monkey when we found Wally. But once we saw him, we couldn't look the other way. Curled up and alone in the corner of a pathetically small cage in a New York pet shop, he kept his hands held protectively over his head as if he were expecting a blow any moment. There were sores all over his thin, little body, and his coat was matted with feces and food. As I stood in front of the cage, he removed one hand from his head and reached out to me so beseechingly that I almost cried; and when I saw the fear in his eyes, I did. As a veterinarian, I had encountered abused animals before, but never one so inhumanely treated in an allegedly reputable pet store. Squirrel monkeys hang out in groups, they hold each other, they need each other, especially as youngsters. Isolated and mistreated, as this one obviously was, he wouldn't survive for long.

My husband, James, and I knew what we had to do, even

though our practical selves said we shouldn't do it. But there was no way we were leaving that little guy behind. So, despite having three very territorial cats already ensconced in our apartment, we brought Wally home.

One of our cats, Croten, a long, sleek Devon rex, was a very nurturing male. So nurturing, in fact, that he was a kind of "Mr. Mom." Whenever a new cat entered our family, he would adopt it (take it under his paw, so to speak). And when Wally arrived, despite the difference in their species, Crotie adopted him, too.

Croten somehow sensed Wally's need for closeness and right from the start stayed with him almost all the time. Before long, they were virtually inseparable. Either Wally would follow Croten around the apartment or Croten would seek out Wally. I'm not sure on what level they communicated, but there was no doubt that *they* communicated—and that they were in love.

For the next three years, day in and day out, they slept together, ate together, played together, and bonded in a truly amazing way. Both of them were equally possessive of the other. If, when they were together, I wanted to take Wally away, Croten would put his body between us to block me; sometimes he'd even arch his back and hiss. And you couldn't touch Croten without Wally's permission. Uh-uh! Croten was Wally's cat. No doubt about it. Visitors who didn't know this learned the hard (and frequently painful) way. Wally would screech, bare his teeth for biting mode, and, essentially, go ballistic until whoever had foolishly tried to pick up Croten thought better of the idea. They always did.

Croten developed stomach cancer. I'd managed to treat the disease and keep him comfortable for more than a year, but I could see that he and I were losing the battle. I knew what had to be done, but I was postponing it as long as in good conscience I could. I told myself I was doing it for Wally.

Those last weeks, Crotie and Wally seemed to cuddle together more than usual. Once in a while, Wally would try to engage his friend in play, but getting little response, he would either scoot quietly away or remain despondently by Crotie's side and stroke his head.

It's never easy, even for a veterinarian, to have to euthanize an animal; it's especially difficult when the animal is your own beloved pet. All that made it bearable for me was that I knew with certainty that I was doing the right thing— though you couldn't tell it from my tears.

I had locked Wally in his cage in the other room during the procedure, but I felt that he was entitled to bid farewell to his friend. Laying out Croten's body on a soft velvet pillow, I let Wally out of his cage. I didn't know what to expect, but I hadn't expected what happened. Wally went straight to Crotie, picked him up in his arms, and started to scream, a keening, screeching, wail. He was beyond consolation and mourned for hours.

Since then, our other cats belong to Wally the way he

once belonged to Croten. He will sit between two of them—with a hand on each of their ears—and you can't pick one up without his permission. It is as if an invisible mantle had been passed. Wally has become the protector, the new Mr. Mom. He is now the beloved guardian of a third generation of cats.

—JANE BICKS, D.V.M.

❧

"But ask now the beasts, and they shall teach thee . . ."

JOB 12:7

WHEN A YOUNG CHIMPANZEE
AND A CRAZY GERMAN SHEPHERD
ARE SIBLINGS, PLAYTIME TAKES ON
A WHOLE NEW MEANING.

Games Primates Play

As if it wasn't enough to be raising a chimpanzee in a Manhattan apartment, we were also at the time parenting Ahab, a German shepherd who was the canine equivalent of a Green Beret battalion. With attitude. This was an animal who considered himself our last line of defense against a uniformly and increasingly hostile world. His barks were as effective as most dogs' bites. No one in our apartment house would come near him. They thought he was vicious, and they hated him. If he hadn't been our dog, I would have, too.

But Boris the chimp and Ahab the berserker shepherd were siblings—albeit by default—and they definitely had a relationship, though the exact nature of it still remains unclear. I could never be sure, for instance, if Ahab simply liked Boris, felt responsible for him, or hated him. Often Boris would run to Ahab, throw his arms around his neck, and hug him, but whether this was meant as an embrace or an attack was also uncertain. Boris, wisely, would split before Ahab had a chance to interpret it. But in many ways, Ahab was like Boris's big brother, and like all younger siblings, Boris emulated him. Regrettably, one of the ways he did so was barking at strangers.

After Boris had been with us for six months, we took to forewarning visitors of the fanfare they'd receive. To walk into our apartment cold was like plunging into a stereo surround-sound megawoofer gone amuck.

When Boris and Ahab played together, ice-cube hockey was one of their favorite sports. Ahab loved to chew ice cubes. Whenever anyone went to the refrigerator, Ahab followed and held them there until they paid him an ice cube. He'd usually nose it around the kitchen floor a bit for fun and then eat it; he ate about 25 ice cubes a day. The hockey game would begin as soon as Ahab began nosing the cube. That was Boris's cue. He'd scoot out from under the kitchen table, snatch the cube, and streak into the hall. Ahab would rage after him. Boris would then fling the cube to the other end of the hall, instantly diverting Ahab. He was really crazy about those cubes. Boris got so secure that he could wait until Ahab was almost upon him before tossing the cube. Sometimes, when he was feeling really macho, Boris managed double plays. He'd cut through the dining room and make it back into the hall to reclaim the ice cube before Ahab could locate it. Then he'd run past Ahab, sporting the prize, sometimes licking it, and fling it in another direction. Often, by the time Ahab got the cube it was no larger than a kernel of corn, but somehow it didn't matter. It wasn't how much he lost, it was how he played the game.

Boris knew he was the baby in the family, and much like human youngsters of similar status, he knew he could get away with plenty, especially with Ahab. He'd often goad Ahab into barking and then race for the protection of my arms, hooting gleefully as Ahab was sternly reprimanded. Boris was so certain we'd protect him from Ahab that he often took malicious liberties.

The worst was his gonadal ambush. It would start innocently. Ahab would be walking around the apartment, minding his own business, and Boris would quietly disappear. Then suddenly Boris would spring out from behind a chair, dive daringly between Ahab's legs, swat the dog's testicles, and quickly leap out of jaw shot in a single bound. Boris would then remain in the safety of whatever high ground he'd gained, while Ahab stormed through the apartment. But no sooner had Ahab calmed down and forgotten the incident than Boris, if we didn't intercept him, would be as ready as ever to launch another attack.

Perhaps the most fun they had together was playing football. Boris would walk up to Ahab waving his miniature football under the dog's nose. Ahab would lunge for the ball, take it from Boris, and run around with it. Then he'd bring it back, drop it on the floor between them, and wait. The object was to see if Boris could get the ball in his hand before Ahab got Boris's hand or the ball in his mouth. They'd circle the ball, feint at it. If Boris managed to snatch it, he'd run for cover and hurl it away from himself (note the similarity to ice-cube hockey) when Ahab got too close. Ahab truly enjoyed the game, for he liked nothing better than to prove his mouth was quicker than anyone's hand. Most of our guests accepted this on faith, especially when Ahab would drop a chewing toy on their laps and dare them to beat him to it. Boris was a lot braver than most humans when it came to challenging Ahab. But then, not many of our friends could scale a pole lamp in four seconds flat.

Boris preferred playmates, but he had pretty good times by himself, too. One of his most pleasurable solitary pursuits was Beat the Sock. This was an ingenious game that required skill, coordination, courage—and a sock. Boris would take a sock and climb almost to the top of his cage. He'd hang there for a long moment, look down, look up, make quick calculations, then hurl the sock upward and simultaneously release his hold on the cage and drop to the floor, trying to Beat the Sock. He'd play the game over and over again. Finally, he got to the point where he could not only Beat the Sock but catch it. It was a showstopper! The only one it failed to impress was Ahab, but I suspect that was just sibling jealousy.

❧

*"Those who think the first year of anything is the hardest
have never lived with a chimpanzee."*

—HESTER MUNDIS

The Black Sheep in Our Family

For a while when we ran our bed-and-breakfast, my husband, Tom, and I decided to have animals on our farm, mostly to give the place a sort of "Old MacDonald" look that the tourists who came up from the city might enjoy. We had gotten several sheep from a nearby farm at a really good price because they were kind of old, but they were fine for our purposes.

One sheep, we called her Grandma, was the matriarch of the flock. This was a ewe who was definitely ready-for-retirement, but, evidently, she didn't think so. Though really much too old to have another lamb—to say nothing of having had more than her fair share in her prime—she got pregnant again anyway. The night she was due, I was worried and went down to the barn to make sure she was all right. As I feared, she wasn't. It was clear that she was having a hard time delivering. A really hard time. I had to help her, and though I could see she was grateful, I could also see that she knew this birth was different from her others. I think she knew that this was the last baby she would bring into the world. Still, she was determined to do it—and with her final breath, she gave birth to a healthy little black ram.

There was nothing more I could do for Grandma except take care of her baby. Through my tears I found I was looking at the cutest newborn lamb I'd ever seen—soft dark wool, inky black, with tiny velvety ears and an adorable silky smooth nose. Now, of course, the problem was how to keep him alive. The small amount of milk I was able to express from Grandma wouldn't last long at all, and none of our other sheep were lactating.

What he needed was colostrum milk (the mother's protein-rich first milk after giving birth). This wasn't something I could just pick up a quart of at the general store, and there weren't a lot of sheep in our area. Luckily, Tom remembered that a neighbor's cow had given birth the day before, so he drove there immediately. A cow wasn't a sheep, but a mom's milk was mom's milk. As it turned out, our hungry little guy didn't seem to mind the substitution a bit.

We named the orphan ram Black Bart. Once his food situation was taken care of, lodging was in order. It was already winter and too cold to leave a baby out in an unheated barn (even if the baby did come with a woolen coat). Tom built a little playpen bed for him. It was a platform with wooden fencing around it. We put a black garbage bag with hay on it inside the pen and put the whole thing in our dining room. Bart loved it.

We started out feeding him with an infant's bottle and worked up to using one of those big three-liter soda bottles with an oversized nipple on it. He would drain one of those in record time and burp contentedly when he was through, which always made us feel good. We continued to feed him until he was able to go out on his own, and I'm still not sure who regretted giving it up more.

We were the only parents Bart knew, and that's how he thought of us. When I would go out to hang clothes on the line, Bart would be right there with me, as close as if he were tethered. When the weather was nice, he would run in and out of the house just like a kid in sheep's clothing, clomping through the dining room into the kitchen to find me.

At the time, we were tapping our maple trees for syrup. Bart thought this was a great adventure. He would follow Tom all through the tap lines and then just jump in the truck with him. Tom would then take him along in the truck on errands, and Bart would sit right up front beside him.

Well, one day, they stopped down at the post office. Tom had just parked the truck when a group of people came by. Bart stuck his head out the window and went "Ba-a-a-a-a." According to Tom, you have never seen a communal double-take like that. All at once, those folks went, "Wha-a-a? A dog that goes 'Ba-a-a-a-a?'" From then on whenever anyone asked Tom what sort of dog Bart was—and when Bart was in the truck they almost always did ask—he would tell them a *sheepdog*.

But little lambs grow up, and Bart grew up to be pretty big. As much as we loved him, we knew it was time for him to make his way in the world on his own. Since we were no longer raising animals, we had to find a new home for him. As it turned out, he was one lucky sheep. A really nice older lady who wasn't able to keep horses anymore but missed having large animals as pets wanted to buy him. She thought he was adorable and would be great company for the sheep she already had. So, Bart not only wound up with an owner who pampers him but with three fetching ewes who follow him everywhere. And though we miss him, we know he couldn't be happier.

—SUE KIZIS

❧

"Thou owest the worm no silk, the beast no hide, the sheep no wool, the cat no perfume."

WILLIAM SHAKESPEARE, ENGLISH PLAYWRIGHT AND POET

Voices

"That terrier just walked the other one around until he knew exactly where to go. I've never seen a relationship like it between two dogs."

MICHAEL FEILER, pound owner in Averley, England, commenting on a Jack Russell stray who became his canine buddy's guide dog when the latter had his eyes removed after being stabbed. (The two were later adopted and now live happily together; "rather like a married couple," according to their new owner.)

❧

"Our dog will only watch television when there are birds on. Our cat couldn't care less."

ROSALIE BURGHER

❧

"Two kittens sleep on my cockatiel Gus's cage. Doesn't faze Gus. He can run around and run over the cats; all they do is kind of look at him. He has no idea that he's taking his life in his feathers."

FRAN CARRUS

Heroes and Saviors

"When an animal loves you, your pulse becomes the drumbeat of its heart."

<small>HEART SONG</small>

IT TAKES A SPECIAL ANIMAL TO REALIZE
THAT YOU'RE IN TROUBLE BEFORE YOU
DO—AND THEN KNOW WHAT TO DO ABOUT
IT. B. J. WAS THAT SPECIAL ANIMAL.

A Perfect Mix—
B. J.

B. J. is part golden retriever and part cocker spaniel—
smartest, dumbest dog I know. We got him from an ad in the
paper. My husband, Mark, wanted a retriever, and I wanted
a cocker spaniel, but they were both too expensive as pure-
breds. So when I saw this ad, cocker-retriever mix, I thought
I'd just take a look. (I now know that there's no such thing
as "just taking a look" at a puppy.)

There were three girls and a boy left, and I wanted a
male. The three girls looked just liked cockers. Then all of a
sudden from around the corner of the room came this absolutely perfect retriever-cocker combination. He had a beautiful coat, an adorable pushed-up little face, and a white nose

with freckles on it; he looked like Charlie Brown. So cute. Mark's old retriever had been named Buddy, so we named this one Buddy Jr.—B. J.

I'm a diabetic. When my blood sugar gets low, I need to get a drink of orange juice or something with sugar to prevent my going into a coma. But when my levels drop at night, I tend to only slightly wake up and just want go back to sleep—which is *not* good. Well, starting when B. J. was about five years old, whenever this happened, he knew it. I don't know how, but he did. He would immediately come and stand beside my side of the bed. First, he'd get right in my face and just stare at me. If I didn't move, he'd start panting *on* my face; after that he'd start whining. If I still didn't get up, he'd put his paws on me—and push. When I'd finally get out of bed, he'd follow me to the kitchen and lie by my feet. He'd wait there until I finished eating and then follow me back into the bedroom. He wouldn't let me out of his sight. But one night, when I was in my first trimester of pregnancy, my blood sugar went down really low to the point where I was unconscious, and B. J. couldn't wake me up.

Mark was next to me, but he's a very heavy sleeper. B. J. immediately began barking loudly right in his face, finally practically standing on him to get him up. Mark knew something was terribly wrong when he was unable to wake me, and quickly called the paramedics. If it hadn't been for B. J. forcing Mark awake, I don't know what would have happened to me and my baby. I have no doubt that he saved my life then and kept me well all those other times when he knew what was better for me than I did.

When we brought our son, Bryce, home from the hospital, B. J. was just waiting to welcome him. As always, he had his tennis ball in his mouth. (I think golden retrievers are born with tennis balls in their mouths.) Without a word from us, he immediately climbed up on the couch, dropped the ball in Bryce's lap, and kissed his face. Right from the get-go, Bryce was his baby, too.

B. J. is now 12 years old. Though I don't have as many low blood sugar reactions as I used to, he is still right there when I do. He is such a cool dog. He does so much and asks so little. I can't believe how lucky we are to have him. I wanted a cocker. Mark wanted a retriever. To find both in one dog was the perfect mix. Somebody was smiling down on us—because B. J. is not just the perfect *mix,* he's just perfect!

—AMANDA ANDERSON

❥

"There is only one smartest dog in the world. Yours."

HEART SONG

August in Alabama

August in Alabama, a thousand miles from home—summer that year was hot and green, overripe with vines spilling out from the compost heap alongside the farmhouse. Eight enormous pecan trees surrounded the space, and across the dry grasses a small barn sat filled with old hay.

All summer long I had gathered animals—strays from along the roadside, unwanted cats left on the land, long-abandoned animals that peered out from the acres of woods. These mixed with the cats and dogs I'd brought from New York City to their first sight of green. But when Harlequin, who had a perfect blend of black-and-white fur across her face and was usually aloof, would not stop her constant rubbing against me, I knew I was in labor. The quick pain that began ended with the birth of my son.

On that day in the barn near the farmhouse, a white-and liver-colored bird dog, a stray I'd named RCA, delivered her puppies, four the color of red-brown clay and one blue-black and white. Summer moved to fall, and RCA tended her puppies as I hung pictures of animals along the freshly painted walls of a room that served as the nursery. A crib rested atop a hundred-year-old table, a curious mix of Southern hardwoods.

The week my husband flew to New York, I fell asleep each night in the big room of the farmhouse beneath the picture window—until the tornado hit, a sudden noise that sucked the glass out from the frame. Rain-driven winds hit the double-hung windows, pressed through the spaces around the closed sashes, and blew straight across the room to the opposite wall.

I quickly gathered my son and all of the bedding into the nursery and stood for a moment staring into the faces of the cats. A last thought of the dogs, and I closed the door of the nursery behind us. Gripping my son in the corner of that room, I watched the water seep slowly under the bedding piled against the door. Somehow the sound of the pecan trees falling was soft and slow.

When the winds died, we walked outside knee-high in mud. Cats emerged safely from their hiding places, but behind the house, the roof of the barn lay where the walls had been. As I neared, the bird dog pulled herself from under, her body shaking with relief. Beneath the broken floorboards, between each joist, she had deposited a puppy, nestled in the straw that was everywhere.

The bluish-black–and–white puppy would become my

son's dog, grow with him in Long Island on an old potato farm, and run the land behind our house that stretched into woods—his mother, RCA, beside him.

—DORIS UMBERS

❧

"God, give to me by your grace what you give to dogs by nature."

MECHTILDA OF MAGDEBERG, THIRTEENTH-CENTURY HERMITRESS

THERE ARE GOOD REASONS WHY CATS
DON'T LIKE WATER, AND SOME FIND OUT
ABOUT THEM THE HARD WAY.

Hero Cat
and Swim Kitty

We lived on a boat for 3½ years with our two cats, Max Atog and Mini Beaner (Beanie). One evening, anchored out next to Cumberland Island, Florida, in the intercoastal waterway, we were preparing dinner with our guests. It was getting dark, and the men were busy cooking on the grill topside while the women were below readying the rest of the meal.

Beanie was doing her usual important job of inspecting every nook and corner inside and outside the boat; she was consummately curious. Max was doing his usual important job of resting on the aft bed gazing out the window; he was a devout dreamer. Both were doing their usual jobs of ignoring one another.

The generator was running and music was playing when the men came below to join us for cocktails, so it was fairly noisy in the cabin. But as everyone was chattering away, there was suddenly this awful and unmistakable howl; a howl the likes of which we had never heard before. And then we heard it again. It was Max!

My husband and I looked at each other and bolted for the aft swim platform. I hit the light, and he ripped open the screen. There, in the dark water was our cat Beanie, crying and swimming as hard as she could against the current trying to reach the platform. My husband gripped the edge railing, reached down, and pulled Beanie, soaked and shaking, out of the water and placed her in my arms. Her little heart was beating as fast and as hard as mine was. A moment later and we would have been too late to save her. If it hadn't been for Max . . . well, we still really don't like to think about it. Needless to say, Max was given special hugs and treats for alerting us to Beanie's perilous situation—though how he managed to give out that heroic, siren-size howl, we'll never know.

We have since given Max and Beanie the nicknames of Hero Cat and Swim Kitty. They still pretty much ignore each other, but I suspect that somehow they're closer than they let on. And while they did enjoy living on our boat, I think that they both are now very happy to spend the rest of their days as landlubbers.

—JACKIE RICKLOFF

WHAT ANIMALS ARE BORN KNOWING OFTEN
TAKES HUMANS MUCH LONGER TO LEARN,
BUT THE REWARDS ARE WORTH THE WAIT.

Just an Old Golden Retriever

I grew up in your average middle-class Jewish home where pets were not available. I never had a pet. There was a lot of plastic on the furniture. Basically, pets were considered dirty, unwanted things. Animals were not part of my experience, so I had no conscience about them.

I got married in 1965, and in 1970 I had a baby. When he was 18 months old, we were living in a bungalow colony in upstate New York while waiting for our home to be built. An elderly woman and her old golden retriever lived next door. I used to see them together when the woman was outside gardening. My son liked the dog, and she was a friendly animal, but that was as far as I was concerned.

When the woman died, her relatives came up, and they emptied her house of her treasures, her clothing, anything they thought of value. They contacted a real estate agent who put a For Sale sign on her property. Then they locked the dog out and drove away.

Because I'd grown up with no conscience about animals, it didn't even cross my mind to say, "Wait a minute. Someone should be taking care of this dog" or "Who is going to be responsible for her?" It just didn't. I was not responsible for the dog.

Some of the neighbors mentioned that they'd feed her occasionally, but the dog mostly stayed near the house where she'd lived, where her owner had died. When the dog would come over to play with my son, Adam, he would feed her cookies; once in a while I would give her some leftovers.

One afternoon I went to get Adam, who'd been outside playing in our yard—a safe, level grassy area—and he was gone. Just gone. I was frantic. I looked for him, and then neighbors helped me look for him. We called the police. For three hours the police looked for him, then they called the state police. The state police brought in helicopters. My husband rushed home from the city. I was hysterical. We could not find Adam. We didn't know if he'd been abducted. We didn't know if he was alive. We could not find him.

The search had been going on for six hours when a neighbor, who'd just returned home, said, "Where is Brandy?"

Brandy? The dog? Why was he asking about the dog?

Someone else said, "Maybe she's with Adam."

What did I know about animals? I said, "Why would she be with Adam? What does that mean?"

One of the troopers recalled that he'd heard a dog barking deep in the woods when they were doing the foot search. And suddenly everybody started to yell "Brandy!" including me.

We heard faint barking and followed the sound.

We found my 18-month-old son, standing up, fast asleep, pressed against the trunk of a tree. Brandy was holding him there with one shoulder. One of her legs was hanging over a 35-foot drop to a stream below.

She must have followed Adam when he wandered off, just as a dog will with a child, and she saw danger. She was a better mother than I; she'd pushed him out of harm's way— and held him there. This was an old dog. Adam was an 18-month-old child. He struggled, I'm sure, but she'd held him there for all those hours. When I picked him up, she collapsed.

As I carried my son back home, sobbing with relief, the trooper carried Brandy. I knew in that instant that she was coming home with me, too. Brandy spent the rest of her life with us, and I loved her completely; she lived to be 17 years old.

From then on, I made it a point to learn everything I could about animals. My focus at the time was old golden retrievers. Obviously, I thought they were the smartest, the best, and there was nothing like them. I started the first golden retriever rescue and have had as many as 35 of them in the house at a time, and it mushroomed from there.

Because of Brandy, I have a calling. I have a reason to get

up in the morning. Because of Brandy, thousands of unwanted animals have been given safe lives. I can't save them all, but I can make a difference. We now have 300 animals—all kinds, including birds and pot-bellied pigs—and are a well-recognized humane animal sanctuary. We take the animals that other shelters won't take—the ones my mother would have said were dirty: the old ones who are incontinent, the blind, the lame, the ugly ones; they're all beautiful to me. So many organizations feel that it's easier to euthanize these animals. I don't agree. How could I? If someone had put an abandoned 11-year-old golden retriever to sleep 29 years ago, I would not have a child. I wouldn't have a son who is the light of my life and who today rescues animals in the state of Florida.

Pets Alive is a life-affirming memorial to Brandy.

—SARA WHALEN

Sara Whalen's animal sanctuary, Pets Alive, is located in Middletown, New York. Even when filled to capacity, they will always make room for an old golden retriever.

❦

*"Blessed is the person who has earned the love
of an old dog."*

SIDNEY JEANNE SEWARD, DOG LOVER

HE WASN'T A CANINE WHO LOVED
TURTLES, BUT HE KNEW WHEN
ONE WAS IN TROUBLE.

A Hero in Spite of Himself

My dog Max was a good watchdog and a faithful companion, but he was also a self-centered keeshond who believed he was superior to, well, everything—especially our other pet, Pandora the turtle. Though the two had grown up in the same household, Max had never shown any interest in her. Not even when he was a puppy, and practically everything from a bird to a worm interested him. Nope, as far as he was concerned, Pandora was little more than a rock that moved. And embarrassingly slowly at that.

Always a bit standoffish, Max became even more so with age. At 14 his primary concerns were naps and mealtimes, and he spent his days shuffling across the yard in our back garden to go from one to the other.

During the summer months, Pandora roamed the back garden freely. Her routine over the years was pretty much the same. She would climb up to a warm rock to sun herself, spend the afternoon nibbling on leaves, then make her way back to her special pool in our yard. We never worried about her because she always managed to get where she wanted to go—eventually. Max, of course, couldn't have cared less. Or so I thought.

One day I was reading in the back garden when I saw Max wake up from his nap and head across the yard toward the tier of rocks where Pandora usually climbed. I was surprised since the rocks were in the opposite direction from his food dish. I was even more surprised when moments later he began to walk up on the rocks. This was something he never did, having once slipped there and landed splayed and humiliated. But there he was on the rocks climbing slowly and determinedly.

Then I saw where he was headed. Pandora had gotten trapped on her back and was pushing her feet frantically in the air, trying futilely to right herself. She must have fallen from one of the ledges and tumbled over. To my amazement, Max went straight to her. With a deftness of motion that I thought him no longer capable of, he nudged the edge of her shell with a swift upswing of his nose and flipped her safely over onto her feet. He then walked casually—and carefully—back to where he had been lying and resumed his nap.

I have no idea how long Pandora had been trapped up there in that helpless position, but I do know that her longevity would have been history had she not been righted. What I will never know though is how Max recognized that she was in trouble, how he figured out what to do to help her, and most important, why after 14 years of ignoring her existence he suddenly decided to save her life. I guess some dogs are heroes in spite of themselves—and Max just happened to be one of them. Pandora and I will always be glad that he was.

He was a very good dog, and we miss him.

—MIEP HAMER

ɔ

"I love a dog. He does nothing for political reasons."

WILL ROGERS, AMERICAN HUMORIST

Voices

"The biggest cat lover in my family is my dog, Sammy."

IRENE SANDERS, whose dog, on three different occasions, found and rescued abandoned kittens from dumpsters

❧

"People say K-9 Solo was only a dog. Yeah, he was . . . He was an ordinary dog who became an exceptional K-9."

OFFICER CHRISTOPHER DONADIO, at a funeral attended by 400 people, 50 K-9 teams, and a five-man honor guard for a German shepherd shot and killed protecting citizens in the line of duty

❧

"Without her, I would have been a widow after two short years of marriage."

JANE FITZWATER-ERNSBERGER, whose husband's courageous Rottweiler partner stopped a prison escapee from fatally wounding him, taking three bullets in the line of duty to save his life

Angels among Us

"Be not forgetful to entertain strangers: for thereby some have entertained angels unawares."

HEBREWS 13:2

THERE ARE THINGS THAT ANIMALS TEACH
US WITHOUT WORDS THAT STAY WITH US
FOREVER.

Winged Spirit

Although I love birds in general, the mockingbird has to be my all-time favorite. This sassy, feisty little creature has given me so many hours of pleasure from the beautiful night-time songs during nesting to the foolhardy but comical bravery displayed when their territory is threatened. I've seen mockingbirds chase dogs, cats, and even people who venture too near their homestead, swooping and diving and refusing to give up while the intruder was still too close. They are smart and aggressive, but friendly.

For 30 years I have been able to call mockingbirds to my kitchen door with a little tick-ticking sound. They know they'll get raisins and grapes when they respond, and they quickly learn that I am a friend. If I don't call them first, they will call to me from the tree outside the door—mimicking the sound I make.

When my oldest daughter, Jennifer, who was affectionately nicknamed Jenny Wren from the nursery rhymes, was six, I sent for a book called *Hand-Taming Wild Birds at the Feeder*. I already had a friendly mockingbird who would sit on the patio outside the French doors until I tossed her some raisins, and this was the bird I wanted to hand-tame.

I started by sitting in a lawn chair on the patio and calling the bird, who came readily. I tossed the raisins on the grass, and she didn't hesitate for a moment in snatching them up. I followed by dropping the raisins near my chair on the patio. A little cagey at first, watching me constantly as I sat very still, she then approached and took the treats. Over the next two days, I put the raisins on a tray table right next to my chair, and she had to land on the table. I think that was the hardest step for her. She had to come so near to my hand, and it took quite a few minutes before her instinctive courage and desire for the raisins overcame her nervousness. After that, it was so easy that I couldn't believe it.

Next, I put my hand on the table with the raisins in my open palm, and she plucked them right off. Then, the big test. I held up my hand with the raisins and called to my friend. She flew around a bit, then landed on my out-stretched hand and took her raisins. I was delighted, and I think my mockingbird was just as pleased.

When Jenny wanted to try it, I instructed her to stay very still and not wave her hand around. She called the bird, and what a thrill it was for her when that little bundle of feathers landed on her small hand and took the fruit. Jenny never forgot it, and she always loved birds.

Some years later, when Jenny was a registered nurse, we teased her about being a "bird nurse" because she resuscitated a robin and a starling that had flown into the window and knocked themselves senseless. When Jenny heard the robin crack against the window, she rushed outside to find him lying still with his beak open but unable to draw a breath. She picked him up and blew gently into his beak. Within minutes the robin recovered and flew off. The same thing happened with the starling.

In the spring of 1989, when our Jenny Wren had turned 26, she was diagnosed with inoperable cancer, and on a fine April morning, just less than a year later, she died at home, which was her wish. I was holding her hand when she left and wondering how such a small hand had enough stretch to play the piano so beautifully. I remembered how the mockingbird ate from it 20 years before . . . and how excited she had been. She had such zest for life, and she hadn't wanted to be isolated from the family, so we had a bed for her in the rec room, which opens directly from the kitchen. She could see the trees and hear the birds singing, with the activity of her family and her German shepherd all around her.

Shortly after she died, while we were awaiting the funeral director, I heard a rustling sound from the living room. I went to investigate, and it was the strangest moment I can recall. A tiny bird had gotten into the house through the dog access. As I opened the doors and gently ushered the bird to freedom, I saw it was a wren. It was like a message from Jenny that even though she had to leave, she was still with us.

I later discovered that the wren had built a nest in a cooler hung on the wall outside. When the wren returned the following spring, I was happy to see her. She seemed to be a symbol of rebirth and resurrection, and the comfort of knowing that our own Jenny Wren would always be with us in spirit and in our hearts.

"DEDICATED TO ALL THE LIVES, LITTLE AND BIG, THAT JENNY TOUCHED."
—JEANNE B. FLETCHER

❥

"The birds know when the friend they love is nigh."

JONES VERY, AMERICAN POET

WHEN YOU LIVE HIGH IN THE MOUNTAINS
OF UTAH, YOU NEVER KNOW WHO MIGHT
DROP IN.

When a Neighbor Visits

On the day the hawklet came to visit, I was supposed to be writing. But when the little fellow appeared on my deck, then staggered through the open slider into my living room, the next chapter or two just had to wait until Monday.

He was exhausted, frazzled, dehydrated, and hungry. Smaller than a robin, with slate-blue wings tapering to black, he had a white chest dotted with black spots and dark lines running from the top of his head through his eyes and behind them; his talons were sharp and so was his beak.

I soon found out that this was no hawk. He was a juvenile kestrel, smallest of the falcon species, and he couldn't fly more than 8 to 10 feet at a time. With a good run, he'd get a foot or two off the living room floor.

Strangely, he wasn't frightened. I started out with gloves, but soon I didn't need them. He'd hop right up on my hand, take bits of lean hamburger soaked in water from my fingers, and even snuggle up to my cheek.

My first call was to Hawk Watch; the right thing had to be done for this little guy, and they'd know what to do. By the time I got a call back, and then the series of calls it triggered, my kestrel buddy was sitting on my shoulder, picking at my shirt neck, crawling up and perching on top of my head.

What do falconers get out of their craft? I'm not sure, but this little guy was a real kick. He sat on my fireplace mantel while I tried to work. Now and then he'd let loose with a "kreee, kreee, kreee." That was my signal to bring him more burger and to stroke his breast with my fingertip. I knew I couldn't keep him. The various phone calls from professionals helped confirm his identity, and the plan was simple. Somebody from a raptor rehab center in Salt Lake City would pick him up Sunday morning. Well, it didn't work quite that way.

That evening I had to make a choice. Dinner with a lovely neighbor or stay home with Kes? Hmmm.

After dinner, we were standing on her deck when a fuss arose in another neighbor's yard. By golly, they'd caught Kes's brother in their garage. I took him home.

Kes-2 was a fighter. None of this pal crap for him. He hissed, he leaned back and attacked with those talons; he chomped my glove finger with his needle-sharp beak. But he soon took some waterlogged burger and went to sleep in a box with his brother.

More calls came Sunday morning. Kes-1 was happy sitting on my shoulder and eating his burger. Kes-2 would now sit on my hand and let me stroke his breast. But if I made a sudden movement, he made me pay. That beak was sharp.

Then came the defining phone call. I was informed that kestrels usually leave the nest early. Mom and dad were probably nearby. Kestrel parents often feed their young for a week to a month after they bounce out of home.

"Put them on the low branches of a tree and leave them," I was told. "It's better than putting them into the rehab center. The nest is probably nearby."

Oh yeah, it was. I'd seen this nest under a loose board in my eaves. I thought it had robins. They were kestrels. And they typically have three or four kids!

Kes-1 and Kes-2 spent all day Sunday in an aspen tree by my deck. I saw mom and dad circling the neighborhood, crying the distinctive kestrel cry, but they didn't locate the kids. I checked on them now and then. Kes-1 kept trying to jump on my finger. He'd open his mouth and beg for burger. Kes-2 stared at me from his branch.

"Let them get hungry," I'd been told. "They'll start calling, and the parents will find them."

At 4:00 P.M., I saw either mom or dad atop an adjacent tree. Just after 5:00 P.M., Kes-1 disappeared. Then Kes-2 was gone. It was nervous time. And then I saw him! Kes-1 had found flight and was perched atop a 30-foot pine in the next yard. A parent was sitting nearby.

Wow, what a feeling. All was right with the world. Then

it got better. Kes-3 dropped out of the nest and sat atop the garage. When I walked toward him, he flew strongly away.

That evening, after dinner with my lovely neighbor at my place and a Harry Chapin retrospective on VH-1 that made us tear up a bit, we saw mom fly into a tall aspen, and we could hear a juvenile cry from somewhere in the branches. There was a Kes-4.

So nature took its course, and we all got to know our neighbors, the Kestrel family. Before he left, Kes-1 and I had a long talk.

He's going to come back for a visit now and then.

He promised.

—JIM SCHEFTER

❧

*"God gives every bird its food,
but does not throw it into the nest."*

JOSIAH G. HOLLAND, AMERICAN JOURNALIST

Little Dog

It was Christmas Eve the night the little dog appeared on our doorstep in San Francisco. He was thin and had no collar. He was also incredibly filthy, slightly smelly, and ridiculously adorable. Fred and I were about to go out for the evening and didn't know what to do. We were already late. I didn't know much about dogs—we had four cats and our lease prohibited dogs—but I decided that the least I could do was feed the poor thing. I put down a bowl of cat food on the front steps and we left. Five hours later, there the little guy was waiting for us at the top of the stairs. Tail wagging. Lease or no lease, it was Christmas Eve!

We sneaked him in the house, and he immediately lay down on his belly and started swimming along the floor, sort of pushing off with his hind legs, in the direction of our four neatly assembled cats, who looked totally stunned and none too happy.

The first thing we did was give him a bath. He was very

well-behaved. Remarkably so, considering here were two strangers plopping him into a tub of water and shampooing him. He had this really shaggy coat, and with all that soap he looked like a mop with a tail. Our cats watched from the doorway, looking smug, as if this intruder was getting what he deserved.

Then we made a little bed for him on the floor, and he got right into it. He looked beyond cute. Fred told me not to even think about what I was thinking about.

In the week that followed, we put signs up around the neighborhood saying that we'd found this dog and reported him to the SPCA (Society for the Prevention of Cruelty to Animals) in case anyone called looking for him. We decided not to give Little Dog a name, except Little Dog, because we didn't want to get too attached to him. That's when Fred told me about his childhood dog, Hector. Hector had appeared on the family's doorstep exactly the way Little Dog appeared on ours. And, despite being the most rational person in the universe, Fred was now convinced that Little Dog was the reincarnation of Hector. It was making his decision—and I knew it had to be *his* decision because he was the one who would have to handle most of the training, walking, and hiding of Little Dog—increasingly difficult. But by the end of that week, the decision we both dreaded was made.

Tearfully, we took Little Dog to the SPCA. But we told them that if nobody adopted Little Dog, we'd take him back. (No way would we have let him be put to sleep! If it came to a matter of life or death, Fred and I agreed we'd find a way around the lease.) The SPCA told us not to worry; lovable little dogs were in demand and that this one would be adopted very quickly. It was, I hate to admit, good news and bad news.

Fred visited Little Dog the following afternoon and brought him treats. He visited again the afternoon after that, the next one, and the next. But not quite a week later, Little Dog's cage was empty. The woman at the shelter told us that he had been adopted by a really nice family with a young boy whose dog had been hit by a car right before Christmas— and that this one looked exactly like the one they had lost.

"I've never seen anything like it," she said. "That child took one look at the dog, and the next thing I knew, he was hugging him and the dog was licking his face as if he'd been his all along. His parents were almost in tears." It was certainly understandable; we were, too. That kind of holiday magic doesn't often happen outside Disney films.

We never saw Little Dog with his new family. But I must say I still look for him. And though Fred doesn't admit it, I know that he does, too. Though we didn't get to keep him, I think that the person who needed him most did. Little Dog turned out to be a big Christmas present for all of us.

—LISA RYAN

❧

"My little old dog: A heartbeat at my feet."
EDITH WHARTON, AMERICAN NOVELIST

YOU HAVE TO WONDER WHAT'S UP WHEN
80 NEUTERED RABBITS AND 46 NEUTERED
PIGS JUST KEEP MULTIPLYING.

PigHoppers

I didn't know when we got our 20-acre farm in Clinton, Michigan, that it was going to become an animal sanctuary—but I guess I should have. Both Mark and I had worked for animals in various ways in the past, and I had left my job with an animal lobby organization because I wanted to work hands-on with animals rather than just save them on paper.

Having spent time as a volunteer at a pig sanctuary in Washington, D.C., it became apparent to me that certain animals, particularly rabbits and pigs, were wonderful creatures kept as pets that frequently wound up being abandoned and then left with nowhere to go. Humane shelters deal primarily with dogs and cats, mostly because they really don't have the time or the facilities or the money to care for other animals, which leaves innocent pigs and rabbits to terrible fates.

We started out with four homeless rabbits. These were

what I called Easter rejects—bunnies that looked adorable in the pet shop, probably seemed like great gifts for the kids, but then began to use the carpet as a bathroom and furniture for chew toys and demanded attention from owners who had lost interest as well as patience. I knew there were probably thousands more out there, and I knew we couldn't save them all. I also knew we had to do our best to try.

Then came the pigs. I learned that the sanctuary I had worked at in D.C. had seven piglets that they were unable to keep. Having gained quite a bit of knowledge about these misunderstood animals and their needs from my volunteer work, my course of action was clear. The rabbits were going to have company on our farm. Our PigHoppers sanctuary was born.

It is truly a labor of love, and I think the animals know it. Our rabbit "condos" and two barns are even equipped with radios so they can listen to music. The rabbits prefer classical, particularly Beethoven. When a piece starts, you can sometimes see them relax and close their eyes. It makes me feel really good, too.

Our intention is to *keep* all the animals we take in, give them a permanent home. Rabbits and pigs especially don't do well with a lot of change. They come in here, acclimate, and make friends; they're happy and enjoy their quality of life. We don't want them to be uprooted and have to be taken away again. They've already gone through enough.

We will, occasionally, allow an animal to be adopted, but, in general, we don't. Instead, we keep waiting lists of all sorts of animals that need new homes but that we don't have room for. So when people want to adopt, rather than uprooting one of our animals, I refer them to those on the waiting list.

I do get attached to our animals and call them by name. One of the pigs I'm especially fond of because he lived in our house for a while. His name is Elliot. When he arrived, he was really tiny, maybe not quite 15 pounds, and he would sleep with us in our bedroom. It was fun. No matter who was snoring, we could always blame Elliot.

But then Elliot, like most pigs, got a little aggressive and a lot bigger (60 pounds bigger) and became destructive. We now keep him outside with the other pigs, and he's much happier. And so are we. He still recognizes me and comes when I call him, but there's no doubt that he is where—and with whom—he belongs.

I wish more people would realize that pets are not disposable objects. The animals that are dropped off here really don't require that much. All they want is a place to live, food and water, and a little attention. They teach us that a little kindness is all that anyone really needs—and it doesn't take much to give that out. I'm glad that Mark and I are able to do that.

—LAKE JACOBSON

❧

"Odd things animals. All dogs look up to you. All cats look down to you. Only a pig looks at you as an equal."

WINSTON CHURCHILL, BRITISH PRIME MINISTER

THOUGH WE MAY THINK WE KNOW WHAT'S
BEST FOR AN ANIMAL, NATURE OFTEN
PROVES US WRONG.

Cassie

I was an apprentice falconer when I got Cassie—and very inexperienced. She was a juvenile kestrel that had been rescued and brought to the rehabilitation center after the tree that her nest was in was cut down. All her siblings had escaped, but she had a malformed leg and was probably rejected by her parents. A kestrel with only one functioning foot is at a distinct disadvantage. The rehab center had to amputate her leg—it was that bad—and, so, in addition to being imprinted she didn't have a great chance of survival and was deemed unreleasable.

An imprinted bird thinks it is a human. It also thinks you are a sibling and therefore competition for its food. One of the most common traits of an imprinted bird is that it screams, incessantly. Cassie was definitely imprinted.

Imagine "kleee, kleee, kleee" working with a "kleee, kleee" bird "kleee, kleee" that is constantly "kleee" screaming, even while "kleee, kleee, kleee" it is "kleee, kleee," gulp, "kleee, kleee" eating!

Cassie didn't think twice about attacking me, all the while screaming at me whenever I went into the mews to feed her. The mews I had was quite elaborate and large for a kestrel. It was about 6½ feet tall, 3 feet wide, and 5 feet deep. It enabled me to stand in there and work with her on feeding and handling. Unfortunately, it also enabled her to fly about and dive at me—attacking the very hand that was trying to feed her.

Occasionally, Cassie would latch on to me with her one foot. Not to my hand or face, but on to my sweater or shirt, and she would dangle angrily there, upside down, screaming at me for having *her* food in my hand. I would try to extricate her from my clothing—while avoiding her switching her tiny but painful grip to one of my appendages—and maneuver her to an upright position on my fist, where a normal falcon would perch to eat. Actually, she looked more ridiculous than intimidating when dangling upside down, often causing me to double over laughing, which didn't help much when trying to extract oneself from 12 ounces of feathered fury.

Kestrels are raptors, birds of prey. Unlike dogs or cats, birds of prey grow to tolerate you, to grudgingly accept you as a partner in hunting—if you're lucky and experienced. They never really become pets. If you got one from a nest, thinking, "Oh, I'll start with a young bird, and we'll bond," well, you end up with a worst-case scenario—an imprinted bird. Birds of prey are very, very independent. You can't dominate or bully them, or they'll be gone. And if you are incompetent as a falconer, they'll also be gone.

I'd had Cassie for a few months. The dinnertime attacks had pretty much died off, but she still exhibited the screaming behavior of an imprinted bird. Inexperienced as I was, I had begun flying her to the fist. There had been a wild kestrel visiting around the far end of the backyard for a week or so, but I didn't think anything of it. I figured the other bird was just curious. On this particular day, I thought I would work Cassie off her lead. She was perched on a fence post in the yard. I began swinging the lure when suddenly Cassie looked at me, looked over her shoulder at the visitor, looked back at me—and then just lifted off the fence post with a grace I never had seen before and soared into the wind toward the stranger.

I went all over the neighborhood searching for her, swinging my lure with a tempting piece of mouse tied to it and calling her to the whistle. I was looking—and listening—everywhere for signs of her. I figured that I would have a good chance of tracking her down by listening for her distinctive screaming. Not a peep. I don't know what I expected. It couldn't have been a hard decision for Cassie: Lure or companionship? Captivity or freedom? There have been falconers who've had the same bird for 15 or 16 years. And then there are others who have a different bird each season out of choice, or sometimes because the bird just flies off. It depends on the skill of the falconer and the personality of the bird. Cassie was only a year old, too young to be seeking a mate. But I guess wild animals are never too young to want the company of their own—and freedom.

Cassie taught me that humans still have a lot to learn about how nature finds ways to take care of her own. In my inexperience, I had involuntarily untrained the bird that was allegedly imprinted and sent her back to where she rightly belonged. It was the most rewarding mistake I've ever made.

—ANNE BURNETT

❧

"Bird of the broad and sweeping wing,
thy home is high in heaven."

JAMES GATES PERCIVAL, AUTHOR OF *THE ESSIAC HANDBOOK*

A CORMORANT'S BROKEN WING GAVE A
YOUNG MAN A MISSION—AND THOUSANDS
OF INJURED BIRDS THE CHANCE TO GO
HOME AGAIN.

Seabird Rescue

I've lived on the Pinellas County peninsula on Florida's west coast all of my life. Before World War II, my father, Dr. Ralph D. Heath, was one of the most prominent surgeons that Tampa ever had. In 40 years of practice, he never lost a patient. That boy was good. And though he was a people doctor, not a veterinarian, he had a definite philosophy about the creatures we share the planet with. His philosophy was that if you could put a person back together, you could put an animal—any animal—back together. When I was a kid, we'd find a squirrel that had been hit by a car or an injured reptile or a hurt bird, and my dad would bring it in to his office and show me how to put it back together. And these creatures always lived. My dad was really good.

As I grew up, his philosophy of being able to rescue

something that looked as if it wasn't going to make it was always in the back of mind. After I graduated from college, that philosophy moved to the forefront. Despite my premed studies, I wanted to do something more than just be a medical doctor in the field of wildlife and environment—only I wasn't quite sure what. I found out purely by accident.

On December 3, 1971, I was driving down busy Gulf Boulevard toward St. Petersburg when I saw a little cormorant haplessly limping along the highway; one wing dragging on the ground as he struggled for balance. I pulled over and walked back to him. Frightened, he flip-flopped into the grass, but he couldn't get far. Gently, I picked him up and knew instantly that he needed fixing pretty bad and pretty quick. My father was working in Tampa that day, and I knew he'd be a while getting home, so I wrapped the bird in a blanket and took him to a local veterinarian friend, Dr. Richard Shinn. I knew he was familiar with pet birds, and, like my dad, was a doctor who would never say no to an unusual case. Or to a difficult one.

"Looks like a broken humerus bone," he said. "Where did you find him?"

"Gulf Boulevard."

"Probably hit a power line," he said. "Lots of birds do it; they don't see the wires. Good thing you found him; chances are a cat, dog, or car would have finished him off in a couple of hours if you hadn't."

He put the little bird under anesthesia, aligned the broken bones, and inserted a stainless steel pin in its wing.

When he was finished splinting the wing, he gave the bird back to me.

"I've done my part of the job," he said. "Now it's up to you to see this little guy through his recuperation."

So I did. I named him Maynard and took him home with me to the beachfront acre where my parents and I lived. My mom was used to my bringing home animals, though a wild cormorant was a first. I put him in a box under a warm lamp in our recreation room and then went over to the commercial fishing pier to get him some dinner; leftover bait would suit him just fine.

From then on, every day I'd go down to the fishing piers to pick up fresh bait to feed him. I'd always tell the guys there what I was doing (so they wouldn't charge me tourist prices) and would get discounts on the bait I bought. Good thing, too, because Maynard was a small bird with a big appetite for little fish.

Word of mouth spread up and down the gulf beaches about what I was doing with a hurt cormorant, and pretty soon people began dropping off all sorts of injured birds in boxes at our house. One baitman phoned and asked if I could take in a hurt seagull he'd found under the pier. A few days later a friend showed up with a brown pelican with a lure hooked in its bill. A day later, a cardboard box appeared on our doorstep with a note, "Bird inside: Please help." It was a mourning dove with a lacerated wing.

And then the birds just kept coming. Most of their injuries were from getting hooked by fishermen who usually simply cut the line when they hook a bird. But pollution, accidents, and truly awful human (inhuman) cruelty and abuse caused many others. Soon cages of recuperating birds filled our recreation room and outdoor pens were going up on our one-acre property. Before I knew it, friends and strangers began to volunteer as helpers, and I had launched a seabird sanctuary. Egrets, herons, cranes, songbirds, owls, and even eagles found their way to us—and, remarkably, many of these did it on their own. Often we would discover a pelican or egret limping around our door in the morning, peering up with a look that seemed to say, "Well, they told me this was the place."

Thinking back, many of those wounded birds remain in my memory. Birds like half-blinded Pelican Pat who had appointed herself guardian to a wingless gull, helping it to its feet when it would lose its balance and fall. And Seymour Sites, a great egret whose leg had been mangled by a car swerving into him. We made him a peg leg from a bird perch, tongue depressors, and tape so that one day he could "see more sights"—and, happily, one day he was ready to do just that.

Today, we have between 500 and 600 birds at any one time. An average of 15 to 20 come in a day. The staff does a remarkable job of helping them recuperate, getting them off their feet and back in the air. And we have a 95 percent success ratio.

Unfortunately, Maynard cannot be factored into that success ratio. The break in his wing was very close to the joint between the humerus and radius, and he developed osteoarthritis. Because of this, he was never able to return to his natural habitat. But he was able to live out his life for the next 10 years as the feathered founder and grand old bird of the sanctuary—as well as my very good friend. Ironically, though, his crippling injury turned out to be a lucky break for thousands of other seabirds that we have been able to rescue, repair, rehabilitate, and release to their rightful homes.

I know my dad would be proud.

—RALPH HEATH JR.

The Suncoast Seabird Sanctuary incorporated as a non-profit organization in 1972 and is today staffed by a group of experienced professionals assisted by many volunteers. It has become world renowned for its captive breeding program of Eastern brown pelicans, and carries on its lifesaving mission with the support of bird lovers everywhere.

This diary, kept by a dog named Bobby, is the chronicle of one pet's journey through the Humane Society of Collier County in Florida. The diary could just have easily been written by a cat, but most cats are far too busy to be bothered to keep a diary.

Bobby's Diary

June 2

My family took me for a ride in the car today. I always like to go with my family, but they don't take me very often. I really try to be good. But my family didn't seem very happy today. They did not talk to me during the ride, and they didn't talk to each other either. Soon, we pulled into a parking lot of a place called the Humane Society of Collier County. I've never been here before. I thought it might be a place where we had friends to visit or maybe my family was going to shop here.

We went inside, and someone told us to go into a little room near the entrance. "Someone will be with you in a few minutes," he said. Soon, a pretty young woman came in and asked, "You want to surrender your dog?" I was not sure what that meant. But when my family said they did, I figured it was a good thing. The pretty young woman and my family talked, and I heard my family telling her all about me. I saw the pretty young woman put all this information into a computer. Then, she patted me on the head and told me it would be all right. "We'll take good care of you, Bobby." She started to walk away with me. I turned around, hoping my family would take me with them. But they turned their backs and walked away. Out the door they went—they never looked back. How long are they going to leave me here? Surely they will be back soon.

June 5

I've been here a couple of days now. I wonder when my family is coming back for me. I'm scared. Everything is so different here. But I have met some nice people.

The first day I came, the pretty young woman put me in a kennel. I heard her tell someone that I was isolated until I had a physical. I was not sure what that was, but it sure sounded scary to me. I don't think I ever had one of those before. However, it wasn't too long until the pretty young woman came back and told me it was time. Then, she introduced me to someone named Vet Tech. That's a funny name for a person. Vet Tech was very gentle with me and before too long, she told me I was healthy and could go into the regular kennel. Before she let me go, she said I needed vaccinations. I wasn't sure what that was, but I found out real quick—shots! Then, off we went to the regular kennel.

At the kennel, I met a man (I think his name is Ted) who feeds me and keeps my new home clean. Sometimes he talks to me. He seems very nice, and I think he likes me. I still wonder when my family is coming back to get me.

June 23

I've been here quite a while now. Every afternoon, people come through the kennel and look at me. They look at the other dogs, too. Sometimes they ask if they can take a dog outside to get acquainted with. But no one has taken me out to get acquainted. I heard someone say I was too big. I heard someone else say I was too old. I wish I could tell them what a good dog I am.

Every day people come to take all of us in the kennel outside to play. They all seem to have the same name—Volunteer. That's a funny name. But all the people named Volunteer have been really kind to me. They take me outside where I can sniff around and run. Sometimes they play ball with me. Sometimes they talk to me, and one day Volunteer said, "I hope you get a new home soon."

I know everyone here is taking good care of me, but I wish I had a home and a family of my own. At the shelter, I have to share with all of the other dogs.

July 2

I had a new adventure today, and I made a new friend. One of those people whose name is Volunteer came and said we were going to Pet Therapy. I didn't know what that was, but Volunteer told me it would be fun. Volunteer also introduced me to Peek-a-Boo—a cat! I had never met a cat, and at first I was frightened. But Peek-a-Boo seemed harmless enough, and soon we were on our way in Volunteer's car.

We went for a short ride and then got to a place called Retirement Home. Volunteer took Peek-a-Boo and me inside with her. Everyone seemed to know Volunteer, and I could tell that they were glad to see her. Soon I could see they were glad to see me, too. One of the people who lived there held Peek-a-Boo on her lap. Pretty soon the kitty was purring away. I think that means she is happy.

One of them patted me on my head and said, "I used to have a dog that looked just like you." I could tell that he liked me. I thought that maybe Retirement Home was going to be my new home. But after a while, Volunteer said it was time to go, and Peek-a-Boo and I got in the car. Volunteer was taking us back to the shelter.

August 14

I am beginning to look forward to each day when Ted comes to feed me. He talks to me and tells me that I am a good dog. I am glad to see Volunteer, too, because I know it is time to go out to play. I still go with Volunteer every so often to Pet Therapy, and I think Volunteer likes me. But Volunteer seems disappointed that I am still here. "I wonder why no one has adopted Bobby yet? He is such a nice dog," she said.

Today, I had a new experience. A lady took me to school. I heard someone say she is a Humane Educator. The school was a summer program, they said, and there were lots of boys and girls there. The Humane Educator took another pet from the shelter—a cat named Willy. He was not as friendly as Peek-a-Boo, in fact, he turned his back on me. But the boys and girls seemed very happy to see us, and everyone wanted to play with us. I hoped that one of them would take me home, but I guess they all had pets already, and there was no room for me. One of the boys at the school said he had gotten his dog at the Humane Society.

The Humane Educator told the boys and girls how to be a responsible pet owner. She also told them about spaying and neutering their pets. I'm not sure what that is, but it sounded very important. I don't think Willy was very impressed. He just sat around and looked disdainfully at all of us.

August 23

Today, a very nice family came to the shelter. They looked at all the dogs, and then one of them said, "We would like to see Bobby." Did that mean they liked me? It must have, because they asked to take me outside to get better acquainted. So, out we went. The little boy in the family (I heard his mother call him Michael) threw the ball for me and talked to me a lot. The he asked his mother, "Can I have Bobby?" I didn't hear the answer, but pretty soon Dorothy, the shelter manager, came to get me, and we went to the groomer. Her name is Bonnie. She gave me a bath and brushed me and talked to me. I think she likes me, too. After my bath, Dorothy said I needed an AVID chip, and she gave me a little "shot" on my back, between my shoulders. She said it would help me find my way back home if I got lost. She ran something called a scanner across the chip and wrote down what the scanner said on my records.

August 25

Dorothy, the shelter manager, told me today that I am going to a new home. I am going to live with Michael and his family. I am so happy. But first, I have to be neutered. I didn't know what the was, but Dorothy took me to the Humane Clinic and introduced me to someone named Veterinarian. Veterinarian was very gentle with me, and all the people who worked with Veterinarian were kind to me. They patted my head, and pretty soon I felt so relaxed and secure that I fell asleep.

I woke from my nap, and one of Veterinarian's helpers was stroking me and talking to me. "You're going to be fine, Bobby. You're going to your new home today."

Just about that time, Michael and his parents came into the room. "Are you ready to go to your new home, Bobby?" I was so excited, and I gave the little boy a kiss on his cheek.

Dorothy said, "Goodbye, Bobby. Have a happy life." Other people in the shelter came to tell me goodbye, and they seemed very happy to see me go. "I'm so glad Bobby has a new home," one of them said, and I thought I saw a tear in the corner of her eye.

So we left the shelter, my new family and I. They put me in a crate in the back of their station wagon because they said I would be safe there since there are no seat belts for dogs. Then they took me to my new home.

When we got there, Michael and his parents showed me my new bed, my new bowl for food, and where there would always be a bowl of fresh water for me to drink. They also told me that there were toys for me to play with and a big backyard with a fence so Michael and I could play safely outdoors. When it was time for bed, Michael's mother put me in my bed and turned out the light. I was a little scared, but I was very tired. It had been a busy day.

In a little while, I heard a noise at the door. I looked up and there was Michael. "Be quiet, Bobby," he whispered. "Don't wake Mother. I'm supposed to be asleep." Then Michael laid down beside me, put his arms around me, and said, "Good night, Bobby. I love you. Welcome home."

> "THIS STORY IS DEDICATED TO THE WONDERFUL ANIMALS WHO COME THROUGH OUR SHELTER EACH YEAR— AND TO THE FAMILIES THAT NOW OWN AND LOVE THEM."
>
> —DEBORA T. SHARP

Peek-a-Boo and Willy also have new homes and from all reports are doing very well.

O<small>NCE IN A GREAT WHILE, THERE IS A CAT</small>
<small>SO SPECIAL HE BECOMES A PART OF YOUR</small>
<small>SOUL. Z</small>EKE <small>WAS THAT CAT.</small>

Zeke, Daveisha, and Me

I was living in a garden apartment in a four-story brownstone on 17th Street between 2nd and 3rd Avenues in Manhattan. At the time I was dating Peter, a producer I'd met while doing volunteer work at a Public Radio fund-raising marathon. (What I believed was my civic duty turned out to be one of the best-kept "how to meet . . ." secrets in New York City.)

One evening, as we were finishing dinner, a friend of Peter phoned to say he was on his way over. I thought, what fun, an evening of wit and banter, but I couldn't have been more wrong. When I opened the door, a rather distraught and disheveled young man, with red welts on his face, stood there clutching something inside his coat. Peter was about to make introductions, when the man pulled out two kittens and put them in my arms.

"Oh, no!" I bellowed.

The little girl kitten wiggled out of my arms and scurried along the floor. The boy turned over on his back, put one paw on my face, looked me straight in the eyes, and turned on the purr machine. In the background, I heard Peter's friend saying something about "severe allergies" and "desperate situation." Before I could put my heart back in its place, the boy cat was in my arms, and the man was leaving. "I can't do this!" I cried.

"Please," he said. "Just for tonight. I'll call you in the morning. God bless you. Thank you. I haven't slept in days." His voice faded off into the traffic. He was gone. The cats were seal points, with the most beautiful blue eyes I'd seen in my life. I was gone, too.

Daveisha got pregnant before I had a chance to get her spayed. Peter and I came back from dinner to find Zeke sniffing a valise in my closet. When we looked inside, there was Daveisha sitting on three adorable kittens. She jumped out for air when she saw me, and Zeke sniffed after her. In a moment of really bad timing, he decided to try for a larger family. Peter immediately grabbed him by the neck, turned on a cold shower, and held him under it. He figured it was a universal bringdown for males of all species. Whatever . . . it worked.

I'd been warned that Daveisha (like many young first-mom felines) might try to abdicate her kittens to me—and she did. She took one kitten at a time in her mouth and delivered each in turn to my bed. I stayed up all night returning them one at a time to her assigned crib area. I won. From then on, Daveisha was a model mother. A smart one, too. After about a week, she stopped hissing Zeke away from the kittens, and he became a regular baby-sitting Mr. Mom. It allowed Daveisha to get away for walks and get back in shape. The two of them were great together. But I belonged to Zeke as much as Daveisha did, and we all knew it.

Zeke was good at a lot of things, and really good at training me. One day when I came home, he jumped up on me. I wasn't ready for him, so he fell to the floor. But he didn't give up. The next time he meowed first, then jumped; I got it right the second time. After that, whenever I came home, I would put down whatever I was carrying, tap my chest, and he would leap into my arms.

Forget about how close we were in bed. I could wrap my whole body around him, and he wouldn't move an inch. When I'd turn over, he'd just reposition himself perfectly. And he'd never dream of sleeping at the foot of the bed. He knew where he belonged. He'd find that place between the shoulder and the neck and snuggle in, his paws around my neck.

Zeke was so big in personality that sometimes it seemed as if he filled the whole apartment. My Zeke was a giant. He had a great sense about romance, too. Over the years, the guys in my life came and went, but any time a relationship was nearing its end, Zeke finished it off by getting in the middle. Sometimes he'd know it was over before I did.

After 10 years in an apartment, I finally got a house in the country, and boy did Zeke and Daveisha love it. They caught mice, dug up moles, made friends (even invited another cat in for the day on occasion), fled from raccoons, stuck together, and always protected each other.

A year later, Zeke began to get sick. I cared for him with homeopathy, rather successfully for some time, but I knew time was running out. Then one day, Zeke decided to depart. He entered the hall closet, lay down, and refused to eat or drink. Daveisha had the good sense to leave him alone. Maybe she realized that he needed to heal; maybe she realized that he needed to die. Whatever she knew, it didn't reach me. All I knew was that I couldn't live without him. Not then. Maybe I needed more time to realize that I was going to outlive him.

I talked to him, begged him not to go, and I cried. He just lay there. So I took my pillow, put it in the closet, grabbed a blanket, and slept with my head in that closet for three nights. I had a bowl of water with me and pleaded with him to lick some from my finger. I kept telling him I didn't feel I could go on without him. On the fourth day, he drank the water.

I got the reprieve I needed to pull myself together. Zeke gave us another year after that. He was my one and only. I believe that everyone has a one-cat-of-his-life, one that can never be replaced. One that was so special it becomes a part of your soul. Mine was Zeke.

After he died, I had another nine months to make Daveisha my special cat. I felt guilty about not loving her in the same way that I loved Zeke, but I'm sure she knew because she'd loved him as deeply as I did. I think she would have died much sooner, but I believe she realized that I just couldn't make it on my own right away. So we mourned together. It was like having a mother around who understood the way no one else could. And it made it easier.

Daveisha joined Zeke within the year. I will cherish them both for eternity.

—JILL PAPERNO

💗

"If man could be crossed with the cat, it would improve man, but it would deteriorate the cat."

MARK TWAIN, AMERICAN WRITER

TRUE LOVE MAY NOT BE EVIDENT AT THE
START OF A RELATIONSHIP, BUT THAT MADE
THIS ONE EVEN MORE REMARKABLE.

Confessions of a Cat Hater—Who Got Lucky

I remember most clearly watching our daughter carrying a young kitten down the path leading to my office. Why, I wondered, would Jenny be bringing a cat to me? She knew quite well that I was not fond of cats. Only recently we'd had an argument over her decision to bring a cat into the family. I opposed her—and lost. My grandfather disliked cats, my father disliked cats, and, ever the obedient son, I learned at an early age that cats were sinister, evil, and altogether disreputable animals. They had no legitimate place in the homes of civilized people, I thought.

My question was quickly answered. Jenny had rescued the cat from a severe beating by a group of stick-wielding young ruffians at a nearby trailer park. At first glance, one might think she'd been too late. The cat looked awful. He was emaciated, had numerous sores on his body, and he had a fractured jaw. Obviously, medical attention was needed.

As Jenny held the cat, she reassured him that everything would be all right. And then she said, "Daddy will take you to see Dr. Waggoner."

"Jenny," I said, "you know I don't like cats. Get someone else to take him to the vet."

"I don't have time, Daddy. I'm already late for class." (She was a music student at a local university.) "Oh, Daddy," she continued, almost tearfully, "you don't want him to suffer, do you?"

"Well, no," I replied. (I might not have liked cats, but I wasn't a monster!) "All right," I said reluctantly, "I'll take him to see Dr. Waggoner. But when I bring him back, *you* will be his caregiver. And, when he has recovered, I want *you* to find a home for him." It was a deal, I thought.

Dr. Waggoner was acquainted with my feelings (more accurately, the lack of them) about cats. After expressing amazement that *I* had been chosen to bring this unfortunate feline in for attention, he examined the animal, cleaned his wounds and made a few minor adjustments, then gave me some medicine with instructions to administer it orally two times a day. He said the cat was lucky to be alive, very lucky. "Lucky," I repeated, and the name stuck.

I had never administered medication to a cat before and was surprised by the strength of Lucky's jaws. On my first attempt, he clamped them shut tight and, in effect, said "I ain't taking no medicine for nobody." Fortunately, anticipating this, Dr. Waggoner had showed me how to apply pressure to both sides of the jaw simultaneously, thus forcing the cat's mouth open. I tried again. As the window of opportunity appeared, I stuck the dropper in the little beast's mouth, squeezed the bulb, and the job was done until the next time.

Day followed day and I saw very little change in the Lucky's attitude. Finally, after 10 days, I brought him back to Dr. Waggoner for a follow-up exam. I was dismayed to learn that we needed to continue the treatment for another 10 days. This was not what I wanted to hear, but I had gotten the drill down, and I thought that just maybe Lucky's resistance was becoming a little less savage.

Sometime during the second 10-day period, I noticed a few changes. Lucky would occasionally jump up on my computer desk and lie down on papers that I happened to be working with. Then I noticed that at feeding time he would walk around my ankles and purr very softly. One day he jumped up on the back of my chair and curled up and actually went to sleep for a short while.

As the second 10-day period reached its end, I asked Jenny (who seemed to be suspiciously overwhelmed with her work schedule during this time) if she had found a nice home for Lucky. "Not yet," she said. "I'm still looking." Then casting an eye on Lucky snoozing comfortably on my desk, she said, "It looks to me as though Lucky thinks he has found just the right home."

"Not with me," I said. "You made a promise when I agreed to take him to Dr. Waggoner, now keep that promise and go find this cat a nice home." But Jenny had realized what Lucky had already decided and I had yet to find out, that those four paws of his were right where they wanted to be.

So, true to the devious personality of the cat, Lucky had worked his way into my life and made himself a very important part of my routine. Evidence of this came as I recognized that I actually had started looking for him at the window and listening for his greeting—a very loud purr as he approached the small office building where I worked and he was determined to live.

I even built a small window perch for him (carpeted, no less) and placed a heavy wire screen outside to protect him from the neighborhood dogs. This also made an escape more difficult, if he ever entertained such an idea. These were not steps taken by someone who hated cats. I didn't realize it at the moment, but it soon began to sink in.

It sank in for sure (and forever) when I brought him to the vet for the last checkup with my University of Florida colors, orange and blue ribbons, proudly tied to the door his pet carrier. That's when Dr. Waggoner confessed that Lucky had not needed the second sequence of medication. "Lucky was doing fine," he explained. "You just needed a little extra time for the bonding process to take hold."

—MARSHALL POWERS

The bonding process took a major hold on Marshall Powers, who enjoyed the love and company of Lucky for nearly 10 years. A year after his death, Lucky the cat became co-founder, with Marshall Powers, of the Gato Press. Dedicated to publishing cat-oriented stories designed to educate and enrich young readers, Gato Press now has a series of books about Lucky's adventures in cat heaven. The stories are told from Lucky's point of view—but all are written with the indelible love of a man who discovered the incomparable joy of opening his heart to an animal.

Voices

"I'm not euthanizing this dog. I put him on the table, and he handed me his paw. I don't kill animals who want to shake my hand first."

SUE MCDONOUGH, euthanasia technician
about a cocker spaniel that was subsequently adopted
by an adoring family
(From *Lost and Found* by Elizabeth Hess)

❧

"They have become part of our community life. And since they reflect our spiritual life, they are our ambassadors."

BROTHER MARK OF NEW SKETE, a monastery where
they breed exemplary German shepherds that sleep in the
monks' cells, join them at meals, and wander with them
through the woods

❧

"You can go as small as a gerbil."

LINDA LASKY, canine CPR and pet Heimlich maneuver
instructor, upon giving cardiopulmonary resuscitation
to a Chihuahua

No Map, No Compass, No Problem

"It's remarkable how many animals find their way home from distances of thousands of miles—particularly since none of them ever ask for directions."

HEART SONG

HE WAS PARROT WHO DIDN'T FIND HIS WAY HOME, SO HOME FOUND A WAY TO FIND HIM.

Oscar's Great Adventure

Our three children were grown and had just recently left home when we found ourselves standing in front of the pet store. Looking back, I guess we had a real case of empty-nest syndrome because we were ignoring the puppies and kittens and just staring at this magnificent bird. He was the most beautiful parrot we had ever seen—a yellow-naped Amazon with an almost jelly bean–green body, a small patch of red on the bend of his wings, and a nape the color of a sunny-side-up egg. We couldn't be sure how old he was—and neither could the owner of the pet store—but since nape feathers don't appear until around the age of one (they increase with each molt) we judged him to be about that age. He was definitely young, so we had to seriously consider what we were letting ourselves in for. In the world of parrots, life expectancy can be 50 years or more.

His name was Oscar; it suited him, and he suited us. We

made the commitment. Though parrots are frequently one-person birds, Oscar seemed delighted to have a mom and a dad, although he and my husband, Gene, had the closer relationship. I accepted their special bond as a sort of father-son thing.

Oscar thrived and provided us with endless hours of delight. We took him with us to our auto dealership every day and kept his cage in the garage's waiting room where he talked a blue streak to people waiting for their cars to be serviced. His favorite conversations involved a lot of "hellos," but then that was what everyone always said to *him*.

We hadn't had him too long, perhaps about a year, when we moved to a new home. One June day, Gene was out on our deck fixing something and had Oscar with him. The door to Oscar's cage was open, as it usually was, so Oscar could go in and out. He never flew far. And if Gene would walk away or call him, Oscar would be back in his cage in a blink. But this day, a blue jay was flying around. It must have mistaken Oscar for a hawk because suddenly the jay dive-bombed out of the sky and attacked Oscar. This frightened him, and he took off immediately for the nearest tree. Unfortunately, this was the tree where the blue jay had its nest. In seconds, both momma and poppa blue jay were screeching and viciously attacking Oscar. Terrified, he took flight as fast as he could—and he was gone.

We called him all afternoon and evening. Gene and I didn't know any of our neighbors yet, but they must have thought two nuts had moved into the area. There we were, traipsing through the neighborhood, looking up at the sky, and shouting, "Oscar! Oscar!"

We left his cage out on the deck that night hoping he would return, but in the morning it was still empty. Heartsick, we put a lost parrot notice in the local paper, with a description of Oscar—and a picture (as if there would be a confusion of found parrots in upstate New York). But three more days went by, and there was still no sign of him. By the sixth day, we were losing hope. Parrots don't fly long distances, they travel from tree to tree and stay pretty much in their own territory, still no one had spotted him.

The next afternoon, a man told us that he'd been listening to the radio and heard someone phone in to say that he had found a parrot. The caller lived on the other side of the reservoir, which was quite a distance away from where we were, but he'd taken down the phone number anyway. We called immediately.

The man who answered said the bird was obviously someone's pet and was eating the food they put out for it, but he would not come close enough to be held. That sounded like Oscar to us; as friendly as he was, he didn't like to be handled. We told him we would be right over. That was when he said, "How will I know if the bird really belongs to you?"

A fair question. Parrots are expensive, and anyone could conceivably lay claim to it. Gene said simply, "You'll know!"

When we got there, the man pointed to a tree in his backyard. Sure enough, there perched on a high branch, was our Oscar. He was standing erect, but his face seemed to be covered with blood. I prayed he wasn't too badly injured.

Gene borrowed a ladder, put it against the tree, and brought Oscar's cage up so it rested on a bottom branch. Then he called out, "Oscar, how about going in your cage?"

Well, I don't think he ever moved so fast to get into his cage in his life! He just swooped down, climbed into his cage, and let his wings slump in a sigh of relief. It was as if he were saying, "Boy, am I glad *that's* over!" And he wasn't the only one.

Fortunately, what had looked like blood on his face turned out to be the strawberries that he had eaten to stay alive, and he was none the worse for his adventure.

It's been more than 15 years since then. Oscar still accompanies us to work, delights us daily with his conversations and tricks, and continues to enjoy being able to spend time outside his cage. But not once in all that time has Oscar ever wanted to fly more than a few feathers' lengths from home—his or ours.

—LOU SHEFFER

❥

"Birds undeniably contribute to our pleasure."

ROGER TORY PETERSON, AMERICAN ORNITHOLOGIST

SHE WAS A BORDER COLLIE WHO DIDN'T
BELIEVE IN BOUNDARIES, BUT SHE
FOLLOWED THE MAP OF HER HEART.

The Don't-Fence-Me-In Dog

Gilly was a beautiful black-and-white Border collie with a personality and zest for adventure that would endear her to anyone (well, almost anyone) and, of course, endeared her to a family that absolutely adored her. The problem was that she just would not stay home. And in a manicured suburb like Kenilworth, Illinois, where dogs found off leashes were impounded and their owners royally ticketed, this was a real problem for the McIntosh family.

I guess when my daughter's best friend, Annie McIntosh, and her family fell in love with Gilly, they didn't realize that a Border collie wasn't meant to be a stay-at-home pet. Despite its wonderfully friendly temperament and eagerness for play, it was bred for one purpose and one purpose only— work. Luxuriating in the lazy life of a pampered pet was just not in Gilly's genes, genes that went back to the sheep and cattle dogs that accompanied the Romans into Britain about 100 B.C.; genes that had a serious problem with the concept of staying put. When faced with nothing to do, Gilly would always come up with something. Unfortunately, what she came up with usually involved leaving home and, frequently, a nifty bit of petty larceny as well!

The four-foot fence the family put up to keep Gilly in her own backyard was, as far as she was concerned, nothing more than an amusing diversion. She jumped it with the ease of a gymnast and whenever she felt like it, and she felt like it whenever she was alone.

Off Gilly would go with a purpose and destination firmly in mind. More often than not her purpose was recreational eating, and her destination was a two-mile trek to the Jewel grocery store. There, Gilly would stand waiting for the automatic door to open. The moment opportunity presented itself, she would bolt inside, head for the dog food aisle like an eat-seeking missile, and happily begin chomping down on a bag of kibble.

Customers thought this was cute, but it was not an impression shared by the store manager. He would call the animal control officer, who would then drive over to the Jewel, put Gilly in his truck, take her to the pound, and write up a ticket for the McIntoshes. It happened so often that everyone at the Jewel knew Gilly, and the animal control officer could just whistle, and she would jump happily into the truck on her own.

After their first dozen trips to the pound to retrieve Gilly and pay the fines, the McIntoshes decided they needed a higher fence. They took down the first fence and installed a substantially taller one, feeling that the cost of the new one would be offset by what they would save in fines. For Gilly the extra height was just another challenge, and she vaulted it with ease. Once again, off she would trot for her trips to the Jewel, her kibble snacks, and her subsequent impoundments.

Finally, the McIntoshes invested in an expensive electronic containment system, sort of an invisible fence. It was one that involved Gilly wearing a special collar. The boundary wire was buried, but when the dog approached it, she received a mild electrical stimulus that increased if she went any closer.

Gilly did not like this fence. She couldn't see it, but you could tell that she was determined to defeat it. She would approach the flags that marked the boundary from different angles, amazing concentration in her eyes. The electrical stimulus was a definite deterrent, and for the first month it looked as if the fence was winning. But sometime toward the end of the second month, Gilly figured out that if she jumped high enough (the electronic device only went up four feet) she was home—or rather away from home—free. All it took was a running jump to get up and over what she couldn't see, and she was off on her travels again.

The Jewel grocery store wasn't her only destination. Gilly also made a regular stop at the local high school, visiting, as it turned out, a gym class for special needs children. Somehow she would find her way through the maze of halls as if wearing a homing device and stop at this particular class. Once there, she would go from child to child, letting each one pet her for as long as they liked.

When the school officials would call, the McIntoshes would drive over to pick up Gilly and apologize. Finally, the teacher of the special needs class got very upset and said, "Don't you ever apologize for Gilly. This dog has brought so much joy into the lives of these children it's nothing short of miraculous. They think it's the most wonderful thing when she shows up. And it is. She's done more for them with her visits than any remedial syllabus I know; she's helped these children believe in themselves."

The McIntoshes never apologized for Gilly again. Not even when she would circle the garbage truck and refuse to let it leave the driveway or try to herd a car as if it were a runaway sheep. Not even when she rounded up a pair of miniature poodles and didn't want to let the owner reclaim them.

But Gilly continued to leap her electronic fence and run. After racking up more tickets than any dog in the history of Kenilworth, Annie and her family conceded that their beloved Border collie was trying to tell them something and that perhaps it was time they listened.

After a lot of tears and a lot of inquiries, Annie found Gilly a wonderful home on a ranch in Montana. Within a month, she was herding sheep as if she'd been doing it all her life. In her dreams, I'm sure she had. Gilly is still on the ranch today—happy, unfettered, and loving the wide-open spaces she was meant to enjoy.

—DIANNE HOUSE

"A dog is a bond between strangers."

JOHN STEINBECK, AMERICAN NOVELIST

SHE MIGHT HAVE BEEN A PAMPERED PET,
BUT SHE PROVED SHE COULD TAKE CARE
OF HERSELF.

Park Avenue Pooch

When I was in high school, we had a neurotic but loving miniature brown poodle named Tink. (It was short for Tinkle, which should tell you a bit about her shortcomings.) At the time, we lived in an apartment on Park Avenue and 74th Street in Manhattan. It was a neighborhood where dogs were expected to be as well-groomed as their owners, and they generally were.

My mother had Tink groomed once a month at a parlor on 89th Street and York Avenue. It was a shop that catered to Upper East Side pooches and their owners, acceding to whatever routines their customers preferred. The routine for Tink was simple and didn't vary: When she was ready to come home, the groomer would phone, and my mother would immediately take a taxi to the shop, wait in the cab, and the groomer would personally walk Tink out to the cab on her leash.

Well, one day, my mother went up in a taxi as usual to pick up the dog and a new employee came out—carrying an unleashed Tink. Obviously, this person was unfamiliar with a poodle's natural propensity to take advantage of any opportunity that presented itself. The moment the door to the shop closed behind them, Tink wiggled out of the employee's arms and took off up York Avenue.

My mother screamed, then yelled at the cabdriver, "Follow her!" Suddenly, they were speeding, weaving in and out of traffic, on a hell-bent chase up into Spanish Harlem. The driver, who happened to be Puerto Rican, began shouting some sort of Spanish SOS's out the window. He must have conveyed a real sense of urgency because soon the whole neighborhood was caught up in the spirit of assistance. People from all directions started chasing our poodle-turned-greyhound. She was going nonstop, most likely terrified by the sudden onslaught of well-intentioned strangers now pursuing her with shouts of "¡*Pare*!" and "¡*Venga acá*!"

The driver went through two red lights with his horn blaring, calling out in Spanish to passersby who pointed in the direction of the fleeing dog. Finally, they lost sight of her. The cabdriver stopped and one woman said that she saw a little brown dog heading toward the playground on 115th Street, but there was no way she was going to follow it. Apparently, some sort of "*West Side Story*-esque" gang rumble was in progress. It wasn't a good place for a person or a poodle to be, but the cabdriver was willing to drive by and check it out. When they got there, the playground was empty. They gave up.

That night at dinner, my mom, dad, and I sat around the table and stared at our food. No one spoke. No one was hungry. We ate dutifully and in such silence that we could almost hear each other swallow. Everyone was completely miserable.

As we got up from the table, the house phone rang. It was the doorman downstairs. In the same matter-of-fact tone he used to report that a package had arrived, he said, "Your dog is walking up and down in front of the building."

Tink had made it across God knows how many traffic-filled avenues, past dozens of unfriendly street mutts (two-*and* four-legged), down rows and rows of similar apartment buildings, and found her way home!

When my dad brought her into the house, she immediately slunk down to the floor; the prodigal poodle touched with remorse—and begging forgiveness for being such an imbecile. She looked humble. She looked contrite. She looked exhausted. Then she ate everything she possibly could for about a week.

—KATHY VANBRUNT

"Nature teaches beasts to know their friends."

WILLIAM SHAKESPEARE, ENGLISH PLAYWRIGHT AND POET

HE WAS A DOG WHO KNEW EXACTLY WHAT
HE WANTED AND HOW TO GET IT, THE
SAME WAY HE KNEW WHERE HE WAS GOING
AND HOW TO GET THERE—AND A WHOLE
TOWN LOVED HIM FOR IT.

The Dog Who Owned Glen Cove

Over the years, the Long Island Railroad has seen thousands of commuters come and go on a regular basis, but one in particular has remained unforgettable. His name was Butch. Almost every day for nearly nine years, he took the train from Glen Cove to Oyster Bay to visit his favorite butcher shop. Once there, the owner would give him as many juicy bones as he could handle (and he could handle a lot!), and then he'd catch the train back to Glen Cove. Not an exceptional feat for a hungry commuter, except when the hungry commuter happened to be a 240-pound Saint Bernard.

Butch was, to say the least, a *lot* of dog. Throughout his life, from 1939 to 1948, and even afterward, he gave a lot to a lot of people. Owned by wealthy sportswoman, Anne Miller Mason, widow of newspaper publisher Grey Mason, this massive canine was a natural-born beggar. He wasn't comfortable with "the good life." He preferred roughing it. Every day he took to the streets like a happy hobo, and the whole town loved him for it.

Butch had a regular route for handouts. He would walk up and down the streets of Glen Cove visiting one food establishment after another—from meat market to grocery store to candy store to bar—never going away disappointed. Then, after completing those rounds, he would amble down to the LIRR station and catch his regular train to Oyster Bay and stop by his favorite butcher shop. There was nothing he couldn't—or wouldn't—do to get a free meal.

Butch slept where and when he wanted, too. He'd often nap right on the sidewalk at one of the town's busiest intersections—and no one would disturb him. When he'd decide to take a rest in a store doorway, shoppers would smile as they had to walk around him. If he wanted to get away from the noise, he'd simply slip into the lobby of the local Cove Theater and doze, undisturbed and welcome, in the dark. He was an animal who had captured the heart of a town.

His naps were almost as legendary as his hustling for handouts. He was known to jump into the backseats of cars for a snooze if owners had left windows open or the tops down. One summer evening, Glen Cove's movie projectionist, Edward Russell, had gotten into his open convertible without looking in the backseat. Suddenly, in the mirror, he saw this bearlike creature rising up, and the next thing he knew he had swerved off the road. No one was injured, and Butch just strolled away, but Russell never got into his car without first looking in the backseat again.

He was a remarkable animal; so gentle that children often took rides on his back. The mayor gave him the keys to the city. He was a character who lived life to the fullest and was loved for doing it.

After his death, the Glen Cove Lions Club honored Butch's memory with a plaque at the railroad station. It was a sculpted bronze profile of him with the inscription: "Our Butch . . . He belonged to all of us."

—LOU MISIANO

In 1981, the Glen Cove Lions Club launched an annual "Butch" drive in honor and memory of this noble animal. The proceeds from the sale of "Butch" buttons are used to sponsor a seeing-eye dog for a blind Glen Cove resident.

Today, Butch's memorial plaque resides in Glen Cove High School, with the children of the children he loved and who loved him.

SLOW AND STEADY DOES WIN THE RACE—
EVENTUALLY.

The Shell's Game

Back in the 1950s, there was an article in *American* magazine about a turtle that had been eating a Milford, New Jersey, couple's prized tomatoes. More than a bit displeased by this, the couple, Mr. and Mrs. Wilson Rittenhouse, deported the turtle, forthwith, to a bog about half a mile away. When the turtle returned two weeks later, the dismayed Mr. Rittenhouse marked its shell and took the animal a mile away in another direction. But, again, in just two weeks, the tomato-loving tortoise had returned.

Feeling that enough was enough, Mr. Rittenhouse put the turtle in a box and drove across the Delaware River Bridge into Pennsylvania, continuing on for a total distance of approximately 10 miles, where he once more abandoned his hard-shelled nemesis. Though there were no tomatoes in the immediate vicinity, there was ample food for the animal to eat, and Mr. Rittenhouse drove back home with a clear conscience.

Months and months went by, the tomatoes thrived, and the turtle was forgotten.

Forgotten, but gone?

Four years later, Mrs. Rittenhouse was in the garden and suddenly let out a cry of disbelief. It had taken a while, but sure enough that marked prodigal turtle had found his way home and was once again munching away on the tomatoes. Whether impressed by tenacity, or mellowed by time, Mr. and Mrs. Rittenhouse finally allowed the turtle to remain as a pet. And (in perhaps a bit of guilty repatriation) they even provided it with a small patch of not-so-prized tomatoes of its very own.

❧

". . . and the voice of the turtle is heard in our land . . ."

SONG OF SOLOMON 2:12

Voices

"A cat, named Tomm, traveled 850 miles back home to Seattle, Washington, after disappearing from his owner's friend's apartment in California—a year and a half earlier!"

FROM A UNITED PRESS BULLETIN, CIRCA 1940

"Our dog, Rhett, jumped out of the car on the highway when we were coming home from Florida. We stopped and searched for him for five hours. We finally gave up. When we got home to our house in Newark, New Jersey, three hours later, he was sitting on the stoop."

LEAH CHOSET

"Baron, a poodle given by French author Victor Hugo to the Marquis de Faletans and taken to Moscow, found its way back to Hugo's apartment in Paris, France, traveling 1,500 miles in three months."

FROM *RIPLEY'S BELIEVE IT OR NOT*

In Loving Memory: Tributes, Epitaphs, and Eulogies

"Not the least hard thing to bear when they go from us, these quiet friends, is that they carry away with them so many years of our own lives."

JOHN GALSWORTHY, ENGLISH NOVELIST AND DRAMATIST

Rainbow Bridge

Just this side of heaven is a place called Rainbow Bridge. When an animal dies that has been especially close to someone here, that pet goes to Rainbow Bridge. There are meadows and hills for all of our special friends so they can run and play together. There is plenty of food, water, and sunshine, and our friends are warm and comfortable.

All the animals that had been ill and old are restored to health and vigor. Those who were hurt or maimed are made whole and strong again, just as we remember them in our dreams of days and times gone by. The animals are happy and content, except for one small thing; they each miss someone very special to them, who had to be left behind.

They all run and play together, but the day comes when one suddenly stops and looks into the distance. His bright eyes are intent. His eager body quivers. Suddenly, he begins to run from the group, flying over the green grass, his legs carrying him faster and faster.

You have been spotted, and when you and your special friend finally meet, you cling together in joyous reunion, never to be parted again. The happy kisses rain upon your face; your hands again caress the beloved head, and you look once more into the trusting eyes of your pet, so long gone from your life but never absent from your heart.

Then you cross Rainbow Bridge together.

—AUTHOR UNKNOWN

$10—One Domestic Cat

Scattered bits of litter clung loosely to soft, silky fur. Confined to a huge metal cage, she looked even smaller. Yellow-green eyes penetrated a haunting stare, as though pleading for help. I could hear a loud purring sound as she gently nuzzled against me. Reluctantly, I tore myself away. The last thing I needed in my life was a kitten. For the next few hours, those eyes bothered me.

Constant images of the fat little fur-ball floated within my mind. Her odd array of colors tugged at my heartstrings until I could no longer resist. The old, worn register clanked loudly. I was handed a crinkled cardboard box with a thick handle and a pink receipt that read: "$10—One Domestic Cat."

Years later, my little tortie is not round and plump any longer. Her poking ribs show signs of her sickness. My counter overflows with medications, vitamins, needles, and syringes and a dozen different foods she refuses to eat. Those huge yellow-green eyes penetrate a haunting stare of help once again.

"Please don't leave me," I whisper, burying my face into her frailness, tears soaking her dry, dull coat. "I am losing my most beloved and loyal friend." Some make remarks, "It's only a cat." I tolerate their ignorance, knowing they will never understand the joy of unconditional love.

I still have the worn pink receipt. I keep it in a frame by my bedside: "$10—One Domestic Cat." My heart is broken, but I was blessed. How could I have known she would give back to me a million in love?

"FOR FIFI: 1984–1997"

—GINNY JEAN BRANCATO

In loving memory of Fifi, Ginny Jean Brancato created RainbowsBridge.com. Bereaved animal lovers now have a special place to hold pet memorial services, share stories, preserve memories, and to heal.

❧

"She was just a $10 domestic cat—but her legacy is priceless. God works in mysterious ways, does he not?"

GINNY JEAN BRANCATO, CREATOR OF
RAINBOWSBRIDGE.COM WEB SITE

Mommy's Boy

Speedy was a most unusual chinchilla. He was "Mommy's boy." He knew exactly what time I got home from work every day. My husband returned an hour before me, but Speedy would remain fast asleep until I arrived. I came home about the same time every night, and there he would be—in the corner nearest the front door—waiting. I would always stop, give him a loving scratch, and put my things away. He would then go back to bed until about 8:00 P.M., when it was his normal wake-up time. He just seemed to be content that I was home, where I should be. If I got back late, he would be waiting up for me like an angry parent. He would put that "where-the-heck-have-you-been?" look on his sweet little face. It was funny. For about an hour he would stay (or *try* to stay) miffed, then he would forgive me.

Speedy loved to watch TV. He would push his chew

205

cube up to the corner of the cage and sit on it like a chair and watch with me. He would ride on my shoulder as I cleaned the house every Saturday. Sometimes on Saturday mornings, when I would watch early morning TV, he would sleep cuddled up under my arm as I lay on the couch. I looked forward to going home every day because I knew he would be there waiting for me.

When I was sad, Speedy always seemed to know. He would climb on my arms and squeak softly, nibble my nose, or paw at me. He always cheered me up.

When it was playtime and for some reason I was busy, he would sit in his cage and stare and give me the "evil eye" until I let him out. Once he had the run of the house, he loved to play hard to get. We would chase him, and he wouldn't let us catch him; he thought this was the greatest game. When we tired of playing "chase the chin," he would climb all over us, tug at our hair, nibble our noses lovingly, and try to chew on whatever books were in paw and jaw shot.

If my husband and I had to go out of town for a day or two, we would always put plenty of hay and pellets in his cage—however, he usually went on a "protest fast" when we weren't there. Once, he was so angry that he destroyed his cage (squashing flat a two-story cardboard "condo" my husband had built for him) and threw his hay and pellets everywhere. Even his water bottle was on the floor. When we returned, he was excited to see us but was so angry he would not let us touch him. He turned his back and literally gave us the cold shoulder until he felt that we had paid our penitence for leaving him alone.

I carried pictures of Speedy around with me, and when my friends showed pictures of their children, I pulled out a picture of mine.

One afternoon as I was cooking dinner, I heard a high-pitched squeal that I associated with pain. I went to check on Speedy, and he was sitting in his cage looking at me as if to say, "What's *your* problem?" I went back and finished dinner. That night he didn't want to get out and "run run," as we called it. I wasn't alarmed because sometimes he wasn't in the mood and wanted to be left alone. The next day he acted normal, and that night my husband and I went out to dinner; we got home around 11:00. In the moonlight I could see Speedy lying in the center of the cage. I immediately threw down my purse, turned on the light, and scooped up Speedy.

He was alive, but disoriented. I held him and called all the vets I could get in touch with. As long as I held him, he slept soundly. Every now and then, he would have some sort of seizure. Finally, after two hours of calling around for a vet that had even heard of a pet chinchilla, I found one that would see him—although they admitted that they had never had a chinchilla patient.

So, at 2:00 in the morning I drove more than 52 miles to a vet that specialized in small exotics and birds. I drove at 90 to 100 mph all the way as Speedy slept in my husband's arms. It was the first time my husband didn't complain about my driving like a speed demon.

When the vet tried to examine Speedy's reflexes, she would put him down on the table, and he kept crawling over and getting into my arms. I bawled the whole time. The vet wanted to keep him there for x-rays and to run tests because when she'd put him in a cage for the night, he had a seizure. The next morning, however, we learned that he was up and sitting on top of his box—and he had even eaten. We thought he might be okay.

At this time, the vet was just "observing" him, no tests were being done. But there Speedy was in a cold, lonely cage without his Mommy—in a noisy, unfamiliar clinic with dogs barking, cats meowing, and birds screaming. I was sure he was scared and wondering why I had left him there. I immediately got in the car and drove back to the clinic. But when I got there, they wouldn't let me see him. I had driven 52 miles to be told that the doctor was busy and the staff didn't have the authorization to get my Speedy and let me see him.

This upset me enormously, because I just knew Speedy was feeling abandoned. He was there from Friday to Monday. On Sunday—after my not being able to see him at all—he took a turn for the worse. I called to find out how he was doing (I had been bugging the "stew" out of them) and was told that he wasn't doing well (though they still hadn't run any tests). I finally got to see him on Monday (after driving 52 miles twice that day). They brought him to me wrapped in a towel. His eyes were no longer bright and shiny and full of mischief—they were vacant, cloudy, milky white.

The vet left me alone with Speedy. I stroked his little body and spoke to him softly—telling him how much his Mommy loved him and that I was sorry for leaving him there. He seemed to try to rally and struggled to get up but couldn't. The vet came in, and I told her that I wanted to take him home to let him die in familiar, loving surroundings. It was obvious that nothing was going to be done for him.

The vet wanted to x-ray him and said I could take him home afterward. While she was trying to get the x-ray, he had another seizure and died. I was in the waiting room when it happened. When she came and told me the news, I felt that my very life had been sucked from me. Even the vet was teary-eyed.

I drove home with Speedy beside me in a tiny cardboard box. I stroked the box and talked to him the whole way home. I remember apologizing to him over and over and saying how much I loved him and would miss him. I don't remember driving home—I don't even know how I got home—I just found myself there.

That night my husband and I buried Speedy under a baby pine tree. I sprinkled raisins on his grave. To this day, I still go out on occasion and leave raisins there. I have noticed the wild rabbits have been enjoying the raisins, and somehow that helps heal the hurt. The baby pine tree that Speedy is buried under has grown rapidly, and now he will be sleeping in the shade. I have never gotten over his loss and can't stop crying when I think of him.

I have two pet chinchillas now, but it's not the same. I have never felt about an animal the way I did about Speedy, and I don't believe I ever will. It is so hard to let go, to love like that again. It is remarkable how a little ball of mischievous fluff can get to you. Animals bring happiness to you while they are alive, make the stress of the day melt away, and provide such wonderful unconditional love. When they are gone, there is an emptiness that goes beyond sadness—but you've been blessed if once in your life they were there.

—CHERRI SIMONDS

"What is man without the beasts? If all beasts were gone,
men would die from a great loneliness of spirit.
For whatever happens to the beasts soon happens to man.
All things are connected."

CHIEF SEATTLE, MID-NINETEENTH-CENTURY LEADER OF THE
SUQUAMISH TRIBE IN WASHINGTON

In Memoriam: Brandy

Every sports team needs a mascot to bring it good luck, but sometimes a company can benefit from one as well— especially if the mascot in question has four legs, a wagging tail, and a pair of adoring eyes. This past June, *Spotlight*'s office dog, Brandy, passed away. For the past 10 years, the pup owned by associate publisher Peter Meadow had become *our* dog as well. Brandy made her weekday home in the reception area of Meadow Publications, a constant in what can often be a hectic environment. Yes, she had doggie breath, and office visitors not used to her takeover technique often tripped over the "rug" in the hall. But when she rolled over at your feet to offer her warm, furry belly, it was fairly easy to forgive her.

Brandy didn't discriminate. She treated everyone equally,

from CEOs to the UPS man. She once refused to give up "her" chair to an important American Express executive. Priorities were priorities, and Brandy's were her own.

Even if she only visited your desk to beg for food (sometimes even stealing it outright in an opportune moment), everyone appreciated the delight that this dog could bring. Feeling her cold nose nudge your elbow while you were busy typing was the perfect cue to rest your eyes and focus on the simple pleasure of petting her.

Brandy was an unsung staff member. We all thought of her as our dog—which for all of us she was—and we miss her very much. Even though every day was a vacation day for this canine living a dog's life, life at *Spotlight* just won't be as bright without her.

—ALONNA S. FRIEDMAN

❧

"Dogs' lives are too short. Their only fault really."

AGNES SLIGH TURNBULL, AMERICAN WRITER

THIS WAS JUST A LITTLE STAFF MEMO—
BUT IT BESPEAKS VOLUMES.

Note to Delta Staff

Ben

Benny, my sweet little rat boy,
passed on in spirit Wednesday June 24th.
He was with me all day
which is what I wanted
so he wouldn't be frightened.
He struggled to breathe and
I'd like to think my touch comforted him.
I would like to thank you all.
It made me very happy
that he had so many friends
to feed him, talk to him, love him or just say hi
in this last part of his life.
I am grateful for your caring.
I am also grateful for the

caring and sensitivity you showed me
as I held him and tried to keep working.
The opportunity to share in his life and death
as just another of life's journeys
without distance and silence
was greatly appreciated.
I Thank You,
Tasha!

Ben was/is a very special domestic rat, who lived to be six years old (in people years this would be in the nineties). Once I started working at the Delta Society in November 1997, Ben accompanied me to work every day, and I saw him enjoy the attention and friendships that he and different staff developed. He ate like a prince and was massaged and sweetly talked to, which made his geriatric time, and me, richer for it.

—TASHA GROOSZ

ANIMALS CAN UNDERSTAND DIFFICULT
DECISIONS INSTINCTIVELY, WHICH IS WHY
IT IS OFTEN IN THEIR NATURE TO MAKE
THEM EASIER.

Chipper Beach— A Eulogy

*Do a Kind Deed and think about doing
it a little more often. You never know—
you might not get the chance again.*

My companion Chipper died yesterday. She was 12½
years old—12½ years of blind loyalty, dedication, and
holding to the belief that all people are good and anything is
edible.

She was much like myself in many ways. Those who
know me well know that every once in a while I do something with no expectation of return. Many wonder why I
take precious time or expense to do these things. It's really

simple. It's because it's the right thing to do. Can't you remember some time in your life when someone did something for you that made you wonder why that person did it? Maybe there wasn't any reason or rationale other than as we go through life someone needs to go out and do the good deeds. The reward is in having helped another.

Chipper reminded me of that through her own selfless act.

For many months Chipper had been battling cancer. We did all we could. The very best of medical attention, surgery, three rounds of chemotherapy, far too many trips to the Emergency Animal Hospital at all hours of the night. She endured it bravely. This is more than I can say for myself.

But despite all our efforts, her condition began to deteriorate more and more rapidly. She would be better for a time, but even then not as good as the time before. A few days ago, I made the agonizing decision to put her to sleep. It was one of the most difficult and painful decisions of my life.

On her last day, I took her to the beach; she always loved the beach. I wasn't sure if she had the strength to go, but I knew she'd want to, and I had to try. We had a wonderful time. We walked a bit, stopped to watch the waves, then took a few more steps. Eventually, we both laid down in the sand, and we talked. I told her that I had to make a difficult decision, hoped that she would understand, and thanked her for all the wonderful years. She quietly listened. After a while, we started to walk back to the car. Halfway there, Chipper collapsed.

I carried her the rest of the way, and when we reached the car, she stopped breathing; her heart stilled while I was holding her for the last time both of us were in this world. She was in no pain. And with her leaving, she had taken the pain from me before we had to make that final trip to the vet.

It was a selfless act.

Maybe we all can learn a lesson and once in a while remember the good things we need to do in life, as Chipper did with her last act.

If you ever head over to Half Moon Bay, take time to visit a most beautiful and special beach. It's less than a mile south from the Main Street intersection on Highway 1. There's a sign that says "Coastal Access." Turn on Poplar Street. Drive slow, the road is not all that well-marked. The views from the bluff are magnificent, and the sand is warm and wonderful.

It's called Chipper Beach.

—STEVE CHAN

"You think dogs will not be in heaven? I tell you, they will be there long before any of us."

ROBERT LOUIS STEVENSON, SCOTTISH AUTHOR

WHEN TWO CATS THAT AN EIGHT-YEAR-OLD
BOY HAS KNOWN FROM BIRTH DIE, IT'S NO
LAUGHING MATTER. BUT THIS POSTMORTEM
MISSIVE MAY MAKE YOU SMILE.

A Letter to Cat Heaven

Dear Sherlock and Shadow,

*I didn't know where to send this, so I addressed it to
Cat Heaven, a part of regular People Heaven. I know
you miss us, but now you have a lot of cat company.
Maybe you'll get to be friends with some famous people's
dead cats, like George Washington's and Abraham Lincoln's, and other presidents who had dead cats.*

*And you'll get petted all the time in Cat Heaven. And
you can lick all the dishes and sleep on the couch, and
no one will ever declaw you or give you a bath. I'm
sorry for the times that I gave you a bath, but Mom
said you started to smell.*

*If you're wondering why I'm writing you, it was Mom's
idea because I was crying so much, and she said it*

would make me feel better to remember you, but I'm still sad. I want to tell you guys about all the stuff we did together in case you forgot when you died. Here is the stuff I remember:

❧ *I don't exactly remember this, but Mom and Dad tell me that when I was a baby, they put you into my crib, and you liked to kiss me.*

❧ *One time when I was playing Nintendo in the family room with Dad, all of a sudden some water fell on top of my head. We didn't know where it came from, but then we saw you guys coming down from the attic, and it turned out one of you had peed on me from up there.*

There's a lot more stuff that I will always remember, but I can't think of it right now.

Love, your master,

Max

P.S. I'm sorry for the baths those times, but you guys did sort of smell a little. Sometimes even a little more.

—MAX BORENSTEIN

❧

"No heaven will not ever Heaven be;
unless my cats are there to welcome me."

ANONYMOUS

IF AN ANIMAL COULD WRITE A POEM, IT
MIGHT VERY LIKELY BE THIS ONE, WHICH
HAS BEEN PASSED ALONG TO PET OWNERS
THROUGHOUT THE WORLD.

If It Should Be

If it should be, that I grow frail and weak,
And pain should keep me from my sleep,
Then you must do what must be done,
For this, the last battle, can't be won.

You will be sad—I understand,
Don't let your grief then stay your hand.
For this day, more than all the rest,
Your love and friendship stand the test.

We've had so many happy years,
What is to come can hold no fears.
You'd not want to suffer so,
When the time comes, please let me go.

Take me where my needs they'll tend,
Only please, stay with me until the end.
Hold me very firm and speak to me,
Until my eyes can no longer see.

I know in time you too will see,
It is a kindness that you do to me.
Although my tail its last has moved,
From pain and suffering I've been saved.

Don't grieve that it should be you
Who has to decide this thing to do.
We've been so close—we two these years,
Don't let your heart hold any tears.

—ANONYMOUS

❥

"Once you let an animal into your heart,
it will live there forever."

HEART SONG

Voices

*"Chelsea, you were the wind beneath my wings.
My first service dog, giving me back my
independence with loyalty and love. It was 1994
when you left me, but not a day goes by that I
don't think of you and thank God above that you
were a part of my life. I am not alone, I have
three more Dobermans to care for me, love me,
and for me to love back. But, Chelsea, there will
never be anyone who can compare to you and the
devotion to each other we both shared. I love you,
Chelsea, I always will, and we will meet again
one day. Until then, know you are remembered,
loved, and missed very, very much.
You were and still are my hero."*

ANN

♥

*"I'm 11 years old. My dog, Baron, was my friend.
I love him very much. I have asked God to take
care of my dog. I know he will. Baron was not
only my friend but was everything. He would
listen to me sing to him even though I sing bad.*

The worst thing is he died on my father's birthday. Me and my dad think Baron chose this day because that way we can always remember him. I love you, Baron, with all my heart!!"

ASHLEY

"Ariel, our relationship was rarely easy. Your difficulties and mine together built a hard life for some years, but these last three or four have made up for all that went before. In the end, you were my baby boy, my kitty, and it was so hard to let you go. Don't forget that Sinbad is waiting for you to show you the ropes. He'll tell you what to do with mice since you never got the hang of that! I love you."

PRISCILLA

"Kadoodie was the original lap cat; didn't matter whose lap, just any lap was fine with him. The only thing in life that mattered to him was love, and he will be missed so much."

MARILYN

"Frankie, you are missed so much! I wish I knew what happened and why you had to die. There is so much to remember about you and so much that we went through. You are my little champion, and I hope that in your life beyond you are herding all the sheep you want and having lots of fun. You enjoyed that so much and were so good at it. I miss you, baby, be my guardian angel, I need you. I'll take care of your little boy, Mick, as I promised. Have fun with Lady, Dixie, Lucky. Goodbye, pretty girl, you're a good girl as always! We love and miss you. Help us. Love, your family."

AUTHOR UNKNOWN

"Gussy, thank you for opening my heart. You had such mission, such grace. Our hearts are broken, and we miss you so much. I guess that's the pain of loving so fully. I pray you're still watching us; how your eyes never left our vision. You acted as though you needed us, but the truth is we needed you. How do I hold you? How do I let go?"

NANCY AND GEOFF

*

"My Holly came into my life at Christmas, 13 years ago. She chose me when she was just a little fur-ball at the Santa Monica Humane Society. She was a four-month-old little fluff-ball who had been abandoned on the freeway. She barked at me insistently until I came over to her, and she licked me until I had no choice but to tell the worker that she was the one. She sat on my lap all the way home and gazed at me with grateful and adoring eyes. I loved her from that moment on and loved her every day until she died abruptly on December 4. Ironically, she died the very same week I had gotten her. She flunked obedience school twice, never missed an opportunity to escape, and generally had a hard head, a loving heart, and a generous spirit. She was my best friend, my loving companion, and a kind and gentle spirit when I needed one. I will always miss her sense of fun and humor and her unconditional love and adoration. Holly was the best Christmas present I ever gave to myself."

AUTHOR UNKNOWN

"Dear Rex, I remember the first night you stayed with us. You cried for your mother. Soon after that I became your mom. That was 16 years ago. Now I'm the one crying. I miss how you used to wait for me in the window when I came home from work, And how excited you used to get when you would see my car pull up. You were always alert and gentle. It hurt me very much to see you suffer so with the pain of your arthritis. Now I know you are happy and can walk again. You gave me so much and I will always love you. Your woolly toy is in your chair and I promise I will bring it to you when I see you again. Love, Mom."

AUTHOR UNKNOWN

Afterword

In the opening of this book, I acknowledged many of the people who enabled and inspired it to come to fruition. In closing, I'd like to thank some of the animals that did the same.

My sincere appreciation to Nemo for not stepping on the manuscript with his wet paws; Wazzo for not pecking the pages to pieces; Clarabell and Duncan for staying on their home turf; and Jags for agreeing to be confined to her quarters.

I would also like to thank Mary Alice; Freddy; Dixie; Samantha; Rhett; Tasha; Josh; Bubba; Uni; John Thomas; Mombackus; Charlie; Griz; Spike; Veronica; Lulu; Oliver; Nick; Rocky; Oscar; Poirot; Puccini; Renee; Poochie; Coffee; Sam; Barkley; Romeo; Hamlet; and Philip, the bachelor swan of Birchwood Lake, for being there.

Lastly, for the heartfelt memories they will provide forever: Olex; Bruce; Flotski; Annie; Don Juan; Fergie; Simba; Ahab; Orph; Black Olga; Speed; Nicholas; Sunday; Buffy; Door; Window; Ms. Muffin; Toby; Smokey; Chirpie; Tiger; Brown Nose; Goldberg; Boots; and Carmen, my granddaughter, an irresistible bull terrier with an enormous appetite for the finer things in life—gourmet food, designer shoes, expensive furniture—and an unerring aptitude for claiming a nonnegotiable place right in the center of the bed.